# THE
# COMPLETE
# PLAYGROUND BOOK

## ARLENE BRETT, ROBIN C. MOORE, AND EUGENE F. PROVENZO, Jr.

PHOTOGRAPHS BY

MICHAEL CARLEBACH AND ROBIN C. MOORE

 SYRACUSE UNIVERSITY PRESS

Copyright © 1993 by Syracuse University Press
Syracuse, New York 13244-5160

Photographs Copyright © 1993 by Michael Carlebach and Robin C. Moore

First Edition 1993
93  94  95  96  97  98  99        6  5  4  3  2  1

We wish to thank the participants of the Ventilator Assisted Children's camp, run by Miami Children's Hospital under the direction of Moises Simpson, for letting us include photographs in chapter 5 by Michael Carlebach from the camp's annual outing at Doug Barne's Park. Special thanks also go to Amy Jordan Smith and Parrot Jungle and Gardens, Miami, Florida, for allowing us to use their playground for many of our photographs. Finally, thanks to all of the other kids who came out to play.

**Library of Congress Cataloging-in-Publication Data**

Brett, Arlene.
    The complete playground book   /   Arlene Brett, Robin C. Moore, and
Eugene F. Provenzo, Jr.   :   photographs by Michael Carlebach and Robin
C. Moore.
        p.   cm.
    Includes bibliographical references (p.   ) and index.
    ISBN 0-8156-2576-6. —ISBN 0-8156-0271-5 (pbk.)
    1. Playgrounds.   I.  Moore, Robin C.   II.  Provenzo, Eugene F.
III.  Title.
GV423.B74   1993
796′.06′8—dc20                                            92-43598

Manufactured in the United States of America

# CONTENTS

FIGURES     vii

1. **PLAYGROUNDS:** AN INTRODUCTION     1

2. **HISTORICAL DEVELOPMENT AND EVOLUTION OF PLAYGROUNDS**     17

3. **PLAYGROUNDS:** THEORY AND RESEARCH     39

4. **INNOVATIVE PLAYGROUNDS:** AN INTERNATIONAL SURVEY     59

5. **PLAYGROUNDS AND EXCEPTIONAL CHILDREN**     129

6. **PLAYGROUND CONSTRUCTION AND SAFETY**     147

7. **EDUCATIONAL AND RECREATIONAL USES OF PLAYGROUNDS:** AN ACTIVITY APPROACH     157

8. **CONCLUSION:** CALL FOR ACTION     173

APPENDIXES:

A. **INTERNATIONAL ASSOCIATION FOR THE CHILD'S RIGHT TO PLAY (IPA)**     179

B. **IPA DECLARATION OF THE CHILD'S RIGHT TO PLAY**     181

**NOTES**     187

**Arlene Brett,** coauthor of *The Complete Block Book,* is an associate professor in the Department of Teaching and Learning, University of Miami, Coral Gables. **Robin C. Moore** is a professor in the School of Design, North Carolina State University. He is coauthor of *The Play For All Guidelines* and author of *Childhood's Domain: Play and Place in Child Development.* **Eugene F. Provenzo, Jr.,** has written a number of books on history and education and is coauthor of *The Complete Block Book* (Syracuse University Press). He is a professor in the Department of Teaching and Learning at the University of Miami, Coral Gables.

# FIGURES

1.1.     Playing alone on the jungle gym.                                    2

1.2.     Shared play experiences on the jungle gym.                          4

1.3.     Neck and neck on the race course.                                   6

1.4.     Going it alone.                                                     8

1.5.     And the winner is!                                                 10

1.6.     Play sculptures as settings for cooperative play.                  12

1.7.     Surveying the landscape.                                           15

2.1.     "View of a play ground for an infant or primary school."           18

2.2.     Children stealing on a New York City street.                       19

2.3.     "Children's playground in Poverty Gap."                            21

2.4.     "Backyard playground in Nurse's Settlement, Henry Street."         23

2.5.     Public school playground in Garrison, Colorado.                    24

2.6.     Indian Point Playground on the Hudson River, 1934.                 25

2.7.     Playground entrance with community building.                       27

2.8.     View from the campfire.                                            28

2.9.     Emdrup provides space for ordinary childhood games.                30

2.10.    View down the "main street" of Emdrup "children's village."        31

2.11.    View across a well-maintained backyard of a beautifully detailed old
         clubhouse.                                                         32

2.12.    View along the outer perimeter of the landscaped berm.             33

| 2.13. | Jacob Riis playground in New York City, 1965. | 35 |
| 2.14. | Another view of the Riis playground. | 36 |
| 3.1. | Exploring the possibilities of play on a timber jungle gym. | 40 |
| 3.2. | Testing oneself on a climbing apparatus. | 42 |
| 3.3. | Developing a new perspective on things. | 45 |
| 3.4. | A nontraditional slide being used as a climbing apparatus. | 46 |
| 3.5. | Head first. | 47 |
| 3.6. | All things must come to an end. | 48 |
| 3.7. | Free play with "qualifications." | 50 |
| 3.8. | The challenge of a climbing net. | 52 |
| 3.9. | An "uplifting" experience. | 54 |
| 4.1. | A playleader works with immigrant Algerian children. | 60 |
| 4.2. | Traditionally structured playgrounds transformed into a multitude of settings. | 62 |
| 4.3. | Bispevangens, a large adventure playground in the Copenhagen district of Ballerup. | 64 |
| 4.4. | Animals are a normal feature of adventure playgrounds. | 65 |
| 4.5. | Small planted areas looked after by children. | 66 |
| 4.6. | Children delight in the creative transformations of cooking. | 68 |
| 4.7. | The Bispevangens stage provides a setting for outdoor community performances. | 69 |
| 4.8. | Legally blind children guide each other around the pathways of the Lady Allen Playground for Children with Special Needs, London. | 70 |
| 4.9. | Provision of low-cost outdoor musical instruments are emphasized on the HAPA playgrounds. | 72 |
| 4.10. | Welcoming tower structure with wind chimes marks the entrance to Flood Park accessible playground. | 73 |
| 4.11. | Flood Park playground provides accessible features to people of all ages. | 74 |
| 4.12. | Accessible water play is a special feature of the Flood Park playground. | 75 |
| 4.13. | A pottery kiln built by children in a Stockholm Playpark. | 76 |

| 4.14. | Parents and children playing together on a simple play structure at Hanegi Playpark, Tokyo. | 77 |
| 4.15. | A playleader and children making traditional Japanese toys from bamboo in Hanegi Playpark, Tokyo. | 78 |
| 4.16. | The inviting entrance to Orrleken Playpark, Karlstad, Sweden. | 80 |
| 4.17. | A temporary child/playleader-constructed hilltop water-play feature at Orrleken Playpark. | 82 |
| 4.18. | Another view of the hilltop water-play feature at Orrleken Playpark. | 83 |
| 4.19. | A well-equipped shop at Orrleken Playpark where young people can work on a variety of play projects. | 84 |
| 4.20. | A "Soapbox Derby" with trollies made by the children at Orrleken Playpark. | 85 |
| 4.21. | A system of undulating pathways bordered by vegetation at Orrleken Playpark provides a complex exploratory environment. | 86 |
| 4.22. | Huge, safe, sand-covered swings area at Orrleken Playpark. | 87 |
| 4.23. | A small playbus in Munich, Germany. | 88 |
| 4.24. | Playbus contents provide neighborhood children with a diversity of play opportunities. | 90 |
| 4.25. | A computer playbus, Munich, Germany. | 92 |
| 4.26. | A water playbus made from an old fire truck. | 93 |
| 4.27. | A simple waterslide extending down a grassy slope. | 94 |
| 4.28. | Karussel, the circus playbus where children produce their own circus programs. | 95 |
| 4.29. | Days of Play, a four-day play event for the whole family in Munich, Germany. | 96 |
| 4.30. | Days of Play, including crafts with traditional indigenous natural materials. | 98 |
| 4.31. | Another activity at Days of Play. | 99 |
| 4.32. | A street in Mini-Munich—always something going on. | 100 |
| 4.33. | The Employment Exchange in Mini-Munich. | 101 |
| 4.34. | Playful City workshop, Raleigh, North Carolina. | 102 |
| 4.35. | High school students construct a "Monument to Clean Air." | 104 |

| 4.36. | Children play on the sidewalk, protected by the *Woonerf* principle. | 105 |
| 4.37. | *Woonerfs* can make a dramatic change to the ambience of city neighborhood streets. | 106 |
| 4.38. | Another view of a *Woonerf*. | 107 |
| 4.39. | Caring for ponies and pony riding are important activities of Dutch Children's Farms and the Youth Farms in Germany. | 108 |
| 4.40. | Planting rice at Maioka Yato Park, near Yokohama, Japan. | 110 |
| 4.41. | Harvesting rice at Maioka Yato Park. | 111 |
| 4.42. | Winter celebration in front of a replica of a stone-age house made from rice stems at Maioka Yato Park. | 112 |
| 4.43. | An urban farm in Birmingham, England. | 114 |
| 4.44. | "Hybernation Festival" at the Farm, San Francisco, USA. | 115 |
| 4.45. | Relaxed community setting at the Open Playground, Dusseldorf, Germany. | 116 |
| 4.46. | In the Open Playground, vegetation is used to stimulate the senses. | 118 |
| 4.47. | In the Open Playground, wild ornamental and food plants are common. | 119 |
| 4.48. | The original Environmental Yard 1.5-acre site before transformation. | 120 |
| 4.49. | Environmental Yard after transformation by the community into a nonformal education site. | 121 |
| 4.50. | Elementary grade students playing and learning at the "river" water feature on the Environmental Yard. | 122 |
| 4.51. | A group of children quietly talking in the bushes of the Environmental Yard. | 123 |
| 4.52. | Children, parents, and teachers working together to transform the playing and learning environment of their school. | 124 |
| 4.53. | Playport, located in Terminal A, Raleigh-Durham International Airport. | 126 |
| 4.54. | Playspace, located in downtown Raleigh, North Carolina. | 127 |
| 5.1. | Making the playground accessible to a child with multiple disabilities. | 130 |

| | | |
|---|---|---|
| 5.2. | Making playgrounds in park-like settings accessible to children using wheelchairs. | 132 |
| 5.3. | Children with and without disabilities meeting on the playground. | 134 |
| 5.4. | A specially adapted swing for children using wheelchairs. | 136 |
| 5.5. | Playground equipment that can be used by a wide range of children. | 138 |
| 5.6. | Playing together. | 142 |
| 5.7. | Dunk shot. | 144 |
| 6.1. | Using a slide in an unintended way. | 150 |
| 6.2. | A climbing apparatus being safely used. | 152 |
| 6.3. | The see-saw, a traditional and often unsafe play apparatus. | 154 |
| 7.1. | Testing one's physical limits. | 161 |
| 7.2. | Hanging around on the jungle gym. | 162 |
| 7.3. | Making it to the top. | 166 |
| 7.4. | Animals in the playground setting. | 168 |
| 7.5. | Getting into the swing of things. | 171 |

# THE COMPLETE PLAYGROUND BOOK

# PLAYGROUNDS

## AN INTRODUCTION

With *The Complete Playground Book* we introduce the reader to not only the historical development and evolution of playgrounds but also current research, innovations in playground design, meeting the needs of exceptional children in playground settings, and ways in which educators, recreation leaders, and parents can use playgrounds for both learning and enjoyment. Finally, we explore the potential of using "safe-haven" playgrounds to improve the education and cultural and social experience of children.

### The Importance of Play

Play is a critical part of all human cultures. Play goes beyond a simple physical or purely biological activity. Instead, it transcends the immediate needs of day-to-day existence by providing meaning and a context for one's actions. According to the great Dutch historian Jan Huizinga, play is "a free activity, experienced as 'make-believe' and situated outside of everyday life, nevertheless capable of totally absorbing the player."[1]

Playgrounds provide a unique setting for children to engage in the play process. Whether a traditional playground, an adventure playground, a designer or creative playground, playgrounds present children with a specifically designed environment whose sole function and purpose is to support and encourage the act of play.

Fig. 1.1.   Playing alone on the jungle gym. *Photograph by Michael Carlebach.*


There are many definitions of *play.* We begin our discussion with one based on the ideas of Huizinga. Assuming that no single definition is complete or exhaustive, we can, perhaps, better understand the meaning of play and its significance for childhood by looking at a range of useful historical and contemporary interpretations of the word.

Traditionally, play has been described as the child's work. For the progressive educator John Dewey, play represents what one enjoys while one is doing it, while work is what one enjoys once one has accomplished it.[2] According to Bruner, play is the principal business of childhood.[3] Johnson and Ershler define play as "behavior that is intrinsically motivated, freely chosen, process-oriented, and pleasurable."[4]

Traditionally, children's play has not been highly valued in American culture. Perhaps because of Puritan roots, Americans tend to think of play as frivolous. As a result they do not adequately appreciate the role that play assumes in the intellectual (cognitive), psychological (affective), and physiological (psychomotor) development of children. Even though play is enjoyable, it is a crucial part of real learning. The value of play needs to be emphasized because of the American culture's failure to recognize the very important role it has in the process of education and learning.

What happens when children play?

1. When children play, they explore a variety of possibilities and ways of achieving goals, which helps them develop problem-solving skills.
2. When children play, they learn to use symbols and think abstractly.
3. When children play, they are freed from externally imposed rules and are allowed to generate their own situations, roles, and rules.
4. When children play, they are given the opportunity to negotiate with each other, learn social skills, and increase their range and use of language.
5. When children play, they learn about the physical world, the objects it contains, and their potential.
6. When children play, they learn to become actively engaged and to give their attention to something.
7. When children play, they have the opportunity to act out situations and to deal with the emotional components of these situations.
8. When children play, they practice and integrate their emerging skills.

Play enhances cognitive, affective, and psychomotor development. Cognitive development includes language, symbolism, mathematical relationships, and scientific principles. Affective development includes social skills such as sharing, assuming responsibility, and cooperating, as well as experiencing emotions such as pleasure and handling strong feelings such as anger. Psychomotor development includes both large and small motor development and coordination. Play helps a child to become a fully functioning person by integrating all aspects of development.

Fig. 1.2.   Shared play experiences on the jungle gym. *Photograph by Michael Carlebach.*

## Dimensions of Play

The two major categories of play are the social dimension and the content dimension.[5] The social dimension refers to the way children become more collaborative and cooperative as they play with adults and with each other. The content dimension refers to the composition of play and what children play with. Both of these dimensions are developmental, that is, new behaviors emerge as children mature. These behaviors operate at multiple levels. Parten, for example, in the early 1930s identified six stages of social participation in children two to five years of age: unoccupied behavior, onlooker behavior, solitary play, parallel play, associative play, and cooperative play.[6]

The content dimension of play can be divided into three basic categories: sensorimotor play, symbolic play, and games with rules.[7] Sensorimotor play, which includes use of senses to discover and explore simple motor skills, begins early in infancy and is dominant until about the age of two. Symbolic play includes the use of play materials to reproduce things children have experienced. Children's symbolic play reflects the experiences they have had. Children from the age of two engage mainly in symbolic play until they reach the age of six or seven, at which time games with rules becomes a dominant theme for some children although others continue to focus on more complex symbolic play.

Another way to categorize play along the content or intellectual dimension was developed by Smilansky in the late 1960s.[8] As part of her work, she identified four categories: functional play, constructive play, sociodramatic play, and games with rules. Functional play is typical of infants and toddlers and includes the simple use of movements. Constructive play is characteristic of children to about three and one-half years of age and includes working toward a goal. In sociodramatic play, children assume roles and use language to pretend. By age seven children reach the highest stage of cognitive play, which is games with rules.

Fig. 1.3.   Neck and neck on the race course. *Photograph by Michael Carlebach.*

## Creative Play

Play contributes significantly to the development of a creative self. It provides opportunities for children to imagine, pretend, and be creative. Simple objects are transformed into props and children become, through the act of play, what they cannot be in real life. Writing about children and their playing with toys, the French essayist Roland Barthes describes how children in the process of playing perform actions that "are not those of a user but those of a demiurge. He creates forms which walk, which roll, he creates life, not property: objects now act by themselves, they are no longer an inert and complicated material in the palm of his hand."[9] Different types of play give children opportunities to make choices and use their own ideas. Because play is voluntary and self-initiated, it promotes freedom and self-expression.

## The Role of Playgrounds in the Play Process

Children's play is characterized by spontaneity, freedom, creativity, discovery, and joy.[10] A playground first should be a place where children can play, use their imaginations, and exercise their bodies.

1. A playground should be safe and provide a setting in which children can engage in constructive and responsible risk taking.
2. A playground should be sufficiently versatile that children at different stages of development can adapt themselves to it to meet their needs.
3. A playground should have equipment, design features, and a variety of settings that allow children to use it in different ways, depending upon their interests and imaginations.
4. A playground should contain settings that can be physically modified by children to support their play needs.
5. A playground should meet the individual needs and requirements of children with exceptional needs.

Fig. 1.4. Going it alone. *Photograph by Michael Carlebach.*

6. A playground should facilitate the process of social interaction not just between peers but across generations.

7. A playground should be aesthetically pleasing. It should attract children and excite them about the possibilities afforded by play.

## American Playgrounds

American playgrounds have traditionally consisted of a concrete or asphalt surface with steel jungle gyms, merry-go-rounds, slides, and swings. Exercise has been the primary purpose of these playgrounds. In general, little or no equipment is provided that will accommodate other types of play such as construction, dramatics, or make-believe.[11] Joe Frost of the University of Texas at Austin — one of the leading researchers in the area of playground design and use — identifies four types of contemporary playgrounds.

1. *Traditional Playgrounds.* These consist of formal playgrounds with steel equipment set in concrete. Typical equipment includes jungle gyms, steel swings, slides, and so forth. Traditional playgrounds emphasize gross motor activities with limited imaginative or creative possibilities available for children.

2. *Designer Playgrounds.* These playgrounds are typically designed by professional architects or designers and include equipment with a wide range of functions. Aesthetic properties are emphasized in this play setting.

3. *Adventure Playgrounds.* These informal, fenced-in playground settings include storage areas and a wide range of scrap materials and tools for children to use in imaginative and constructive play activities. Cooking, gardening, and animal care are some of the activities typically found in adventure playgrounds.

4. *Creative Playgrounds.* These semiformal playgrounds are constructed from existing commercial equipment combined with a wide range of scavenged materials such as telephone poles, railroad ties, and rubber tires. All types of play are encouraged in this setting.[12]

Fig. 1.5.
And the winner is!
*Photograph by Michael Carlebach.*

## Traditional Playgrounds

Traditional playgrounds have increasingly come to be recognized as having severe limitations as play and learning environments. Critics describe them as one-dimensional, lacking in natural landscaping, anchored and constructed to allow only certain types of play, and unresponsive to children's individual needs.[13] Natural forms of play, such as construction and make-believe, are usually not stimulated by traditional playgrounds. From a developmental point of view, the traditional playground ignores many of the critical needs of children.[14]

Unfortunately, traditional playgrounds still dominate American schools, public parks, community centers, and recreation sites. Despite their poor safety record and their failure to allow children to exercise fully their creativity and spontaneity as part of the process of play, they predominate. A number of explanations are possible. Traditional playgrounds are easier to maintain physically than are designer or adventure playgrounds. Aesthetically, traditional playgrounds are more pleasing to many people. They are perceived as better fitting into the architecture of schools and local neighborhoods than designer playgrounds or, particularly, adventure playgrounds. In addition, traditional playgrounds are sometimes perceived as safer than designer or adventure playgrounds. As we discuss in chapter 6, this is a serious misconception but one which, nonetheless, remains widespread. Above all, this backward view of what constitutes a good developmentally oriented playground is the result of both ignorance and a tendency to devalue the importance of children's play on the part of public officials. America's children need much stronger advocates among public decision makers willing to speak out in favor of higher-quality play environments.

Fig. 1.6.   Play sculptures as settings for cooperative play. *Photograph by Michael Carlebach.*

## Designer Playgrounds

Designer playgrounds represent an attempt by the minority, a more enlightened community of advocates (designers, educators, park and recreation professionals, etc.), to provide children with playground settings that more particularly meet their needs and that aesthetically complement the environments in which they are set. The designer playground is sufficiently open and flexible to permit a wider range of activities and experiences than the traditional playground. When designed well, designer playgrounds are significantly safer than traditional playgrounds because the notoriously unsafe features are excluded and full attention is paid to the installation of adequate safety surfaces.

The impetus for the development of designer playgrounds in the United States came out of the late 1960s and early 1970s. Architects such as Paul Friedberg developed a number of highly innovative parks and playgrounds for inner-city New York children. Richard Dattner developed a number of interesting designs, including an "ancient play garden" adjacent to the Egyptian Temple at the Metropolitan Museum of Art. During the 1970s, the Environmental Yard was constructed on the grounds of a Berkeley, California, elementary school. This action research project differed from others of the same era both in the extent to which natural play settings were emphasized and in the integration of the outdoors as a play and learning resource in the school curriculum. Robin Moore, the principal design-researcher, worked closely with the teaching staff. Results from the ten-year research and development effort eventually became the core material for the design book, *Play For All Guidelines*.[15] Other innovative designers from this period include Naud Burnett of Dallas and Ron Hartley of Jackson, Mississippi.[16] Discussions of their work appear in chapter 2.

## Adventure Playgrounds

Adventure playgrounds were first introduced into Denmark during the Second World War. Although extremely popular in many parts of Europe, only a few have been introduced into the United States. In an adventure playground, children work with trained play leaders who give them the opportunity to undertake activities that have traditionally been a part of childhood, such as building huts, walls, and forts, planting gardens, climbing trees, digging holes, creating waterways, dressing up, reading, or just general "messing around," but are increasingly discouraged in densely populated urban settings.[17]

Adventure playgrounds are seen by many people as eyesores and potentially dangerous places for children to play. Undoubtedly, these perceptions have limited their acceptance as models for playgrounds in the United States. Fears concerning children's safety in adventure playgrounds are largely unwarranted. In general, their safety record is significantly better than that of traditional playgrounds.[18] If properly designed with good landscaping, adventure playgrounds can blend in to complement almost any setting. To be acceptable, they must be created through a strong community participation process.

## Creative Playgrounds

To a large extent, creative playgrounds represent a fusion of traditional and designer playgrounds and sometimes include aspects of the adventure playground. The principal purpose of these playgrounds is to provide children with a maximum range of play possibilities at low cost. Because recycled materials and found objects are used, the range of designs for these playgrounds is quite diverse.

Creative playgrounds usually result from a community initiative and are created through a community participation process. A number of American playground builders (Paul Hogan, William Weitz, and Kit Clews) have specialized in this field for more than twenty years. Such playgrounds have quietly sprung up across the country and sometimes are confused in people's minds with adventure playgrounds or are misnamed as adventure playgrounds. When properly designed, these playgrounds are not only safe and aesthetically pleasing but provide a wide range of play options for the children who use them.

Fig. 1.7.
Surveying the landscape.
*Photograph by Michael Carlebach.*

# 2

# HISTORICAL DEVELOPMENT AND EVOLUTION OF PLAYGROUNDS

The early history of playgrounds in the United States remains obscure. Early architectural sources, such as Henry Barnard's 1848 *School Architecture*, include an illustration for a "play ground for an infant or primary school" (fig. 2.1). Describing the illustration, Barnard explains that it

> represents a well regulated playground with all the necessary apparatus. It will be seen that there are two rotary swings, one for the boys the other for the girls. The girls are represented vaulting over a rope, which they sometimes do, as also do the boys. The boys are represented in swinging the usual way, without the vaulting rope. It will be seen that some of the children are represented as engaged in erecting their various buildings; some are building solid oblong pillars, others are busy erecting squares, others pentagons, others hexagons, and so on, as they may feel inclined. The play-ground is flagged, and a little cart is represented, to enable the children to take the wood bricks away, and place them in their proper places, as on no account are they to be left out, when the children are done with.[1]

Fruit trees surround the playground. According to Barnard, the presence of teachers on the playground is "absolutely essential." Not only do they prevent accidents from occurring but they can attend to the moral and physical training of the children under their charge. Although carefully supervised, Barnard, nonetheless, recognizes the importance of free play. He advises, for ex-

Fig. 2.1.  View of a play ground for an infant or primary school. From Henry Barnard, *School Architecture; or Contributions to the Improvement of School-Houses in the United States* (New York: A. S. Barnes, 1848).

ample, that "the pupils being supplied with the necessary articles for amusement, the teacher must not fail to remember that the choice is always left to the children. If they play at what they choose they are free beings, and manifest their characters; but if they are forced to play at what they do not wish, they do not manifest their characters, but are cramped and are slaves, and hence their faculties are not developed."[2]

Barnard's description and illustration of a "play ground" from *School Architecture* is important because it provides a sense of the degree to which playgrounds had evolved by the middle of the nineteenth century. What Barnard, one of the pioneers of the Common School Movement and the most so-

Fig. 2.2.   Children stealing on a New York City street. *Photograph by Jacob Riis (early 1890s). Courtesy Library of Congress.*

phisticated writer on school architecture and design from his era, was describing was essentially a play yard. The modern playground with its swings and slides, teeter-toters, and monkey bars was not created until the early decades of the twentieth century.

According to Clarence Rainwater, one of the early pioneers of playgrounds and the play movement in the United States, an outdoor children's playground was set up in 1868 in Boston under the supervision of the Old First Church in the yard of a public school near Copley Square.[3] Following models developed in Germany during the 1880s, the committee of the Massachusetts Emergency and Hygiene Association at the suggestion of Dr. Marie

Zakrzewska placed piles of sand bordered by wooden squares large enough to allow five or six children to play together.[4] Sand yards or sand gardens of the type suggested by Zakrzewska were built in 1886 for the Children's Mission, Parameter Street Chapel, and Warrenton Street Chapel in Boston.[5] By 1887, officials in Boston had approved the construction of ten sand gardens in the city's poorest districts.[6]

The movement to establish public playgrounds in New York City began at approximately the same time as in Boston. In 1887, the city passed legislation that called for the establishment of small parks with playground equipment.[7] The New York law made it possible for the city to spend up to $1 million per year to establish small city parks and playgrounds. Despite the passage of this legislation, the development of playgrounds throughout the city progressed slowly, particularly in the immigrant neighborhoods. The social reformer and journalist Jacob Riis (1849 – 1914), for example, complained in 1892 that "there are no playgrounds yet below Fourteenth Street and room and need for fifty."[8] In his book *The Children of the Poor*, Riis compares the children "who skip among the trees and lawns" with those who "root in the gutters."[9] He emphasized that the street was the only playground available to the children of the tenements, that the street was "an educator with its own plan," and that the plan was "not a safe one."[10] Riis believed that by providing city children with proper playgrounds, they would not only stay out of trouble but that the foundations for a better society would be laid. Ideas such as this clearly complemented those of the German Herbartian movement as well as the theories of the psychologist G. Stanley Hall and the educational philosopher John Dewey. Play represented a civilizing force in the education of the child.

In New York City, figures such as Riis criticized the failure of the Small Parks Law. Despite the appropriation of millions of dollars in city funds in the seven years following the passage of the law, no playgrounds had been built. As part of renewed reform efforts in 1894, Riis proposed that sufficient land be condemned around every public school in the city so that a park could be established. Besides serving the needs of the schools, these parks would also serve the needs of the neighborhoods. As Riis explained, "My school-park should be a people's park in which the children might play at recess and where

Fig. 2.3. "Children's playground in Poverty Gap." *Photograph by Jacob Riis (ca. 1888—1889). Courtesy Library of Congress.*

the mothers might take their babies during school hours. It should always be and there should be plenty of seats in it."[11] One of the first playgrounds to be established as a result of Riis's efforts was in Poverty Gap. Although limited, if judged by contemporary standards, it was an important beginning and represents one of the earliest examples of the playground as a vehicle of social improvement (fig. 2.3).

Riis in his efforts at playground reform was part of a larger social reform movement concerned with improving the conditions of the urban poor. As did Jane Addams at Hull House in Chicago, he worked to create a social and cultural environment within the city that would preserve the dignity of the poor and strengthen the bonds of the family. The development of community-oriented public schools and neighborhood parks and playgrounds was crucial to his plans.

A sand garden type of playground was opened by Jane Addams in 1894 in Chicago on land contributed by William Kent. This playground was open to both children and youths and took up approximately three-quarters of an acre. A sand pile, swings, building blocks, and a giant stride were provided for the children who used the playground. An experienced kindergarten teacher and a police officer provided different types of supervision on the playground.[12]

In 1896, a second playground was started in Chicago as part of the Northwestern University Settlement, and in 1898, a third public playground was opened by the University of Chicago.[13] Similar playgrounds to those set up in New York, Boston, and Chicago began to come into widespread use in other cities around the country (fig. 2.4). By contemporary standards these playgrounds were relatively limited. Equipment consisted of little more than swings and sand piles. Despite limitations, they provided an important alternative for children and their play where few such opportunities had existed before.

## "Organized" Play as a Social Movement

As a direct result of the increase in urban playgrounds in the United States during the late nineteenth century, a national "play movement" developed. Under the auspices of the Playground Association of America, which was founded in 1906, figures such as Joseph Lee, Jane Addams, and J. G. Phelps Stokes pursued the development of "organized play" for American children (figs. 2.5, 2.6). The purpose of the movement was to structure the play experience of American youth on well-equipped municipal playgrounds. Contemporary the-

Fig. 2.4. "Backyard playground in Nurse's Settlement, Henry Street." *Photograph by Jacob Riis (late 1890s). Courtesy Library of Congress.*

orists such as Dominick Cavallo have argued that this movement toward organized and controlled play on the part of local municipal governments represented a conscious attempt to control the lives and experiences of urban youths. According to him, "Inviting young people to use organized playgrounds was more than a strategy for removing them from parental supervision or providing them with healthy exercise. Modern biological and psycho-

Fig. 2.5.  Public school playground in Garrison, Colorado, showing both free and organized play. *Photograph by J. H. Pankratz, November 1913. Courtesy Library of Congress.*

logical theories of child development had convinced play advocates that playground experiences were means through which the young developed specific cognitive skills, moral tendencies and social values."[14] The activities on the playground were seen as critically shaping the personality and morals of the child. Essentially, play and playground activities came to be viewed as means of socialization.[15] Through playground activities, children would learn to become team players. The activities developed by play organizers during the decades immediately preceding the First World War "emphasized a consensual approach to social interactions."[16] Rules were agreed on beforehand and followed. "Team games," according to Cavallo, "symbolized the key goals of modern liberalism: harmony between classes, orderly competition between interest groups, and individual achievement within frameworks of group and social process."[17]

Fig. 2.6.   Indian Point Playground on the Hudson River, 1934. Whitteman Collection. *Courtesy Library of Congress.*

It was during the period before the First World War that the "traditional" playground was largely formulated. In photographs, drawings, and advertisements from this early period, one can see the evolution from relatively crude playground equipment to finished and manufactured apparatus, including swings, teeter-totters, and merry-go'rounds.

In a certain sense, the period preceding the First World War saw the institutionalization of the playground in American society. What represented innovation and reform at the beginning of the century had evolved into a common and expected element of the urban landscape by the 1930s and 1940s.

## Adventure Playgrounds

During the mid-1940s, playgrounds underwent a profound redefinition in Europe with the introduction of Adventure Playgrounds. The adventure playground movement recognized the fundamental need of children to create not only physical but social constructions. An adventure playground, as defined by the London-based Playing Fields Association, is "a place where children of all ages, under friendly supervision, are free to do many things they can no longer easily do in our crowded urban society; things like building huts, walls, forts, dens, treehouses, lighting fires and cooking; tree climbing, digging, camping; perhaps gardening and keeping animals; as well as playing team games, group games, painting, dressing up, modelling, reading . . . or doing nothing."[18]

The origins of adventure playgrounds go back to 1943 when the Danish landscape architect and educator C. Th. Sorenson together with the Workers' Co-operative Association built the first adventure playground at Emdrup outside of Copenhagen. The playground took up an area of approximately seven thousand square meters and was surrounded by six-foot-high banks of earth excavated from the playground site. On top of the bank was placed a wire fence, at the base of which were planted a variety of shrubs forming an impenetrable thicket.[19]

John Bertelsen, who was the director of the playground at Emdrup from 1943 to 1947, contributed much to its philosophy. In an essay reflecting on his experience at Emdrup, Bertelsen outlined his basic philosophy about the role and importance of play to the development of the child.

> Children's play development is closely related to their environment—the physical and the psychical—to adults' and society's attitudes toward play. The children's behavior and play at the adventure playground demonstrated this, and the influence of various conditions was clearly reflected. It is not sufficient for adults and society merely to provide facilities for play—they must offer a positive, individual attitude towards it, so that the physical climate for the child's growth, through play, is created.[20]

Fig. 2.7.  Playground entrance with community building (containing cafe, meeting rooms, and workshop) to the right overlooking a central meadow. *Photograph by Robin Moore.*

For Bertelsen it was essential that a link exist between the physical environment and the psychological environment of the child. For him play had to do with attacking life in an unconventional manner. He felt ultimately that children were gluttons for life and that the adventure playground was an ideal environment in which they could exercise their appetites. (figs. 2.7−2.12).[21]

Fig. 2.8.    View from the campfire, across the meadows to the community building in the background. *Photograph by Robin Moore.*

The spirit of the playground at Emdrup is conveyed by quotes from Bertelsen's diary of his experiences during the first year of the playground's operation. On the day the playground opened, Bertelsen recalled how. "We began by moving all the building material in the open shed. Bricks, boards, fireposts and cement pillars were moved to the left alongside the entrance, where building and digging started right away. The work was done by children aged 4 to 17. It went on at full speed and all the workers were in high spirits; dust, sweat, warning shouts and a few scratches all created just the right atmosphere."[22]

The concept of the adventure playground was introduced into Great Britain immediately following World War II by Lady Allen of Hurtwood who visited the playground at Emdrup and became excited about its possibilities. The destruction of the war created an abundance of "found" objects with which children could build and experiment. It was in Britain that the concept of the adventure playground truly took hold, spreading in time to other parts of Europe and eventually to the United States (fig. 2.5).

Over the years a number of basic values have emerged as part of the adventure playground movement. These have been identified by Bill Michaelis.

1.  At adventure playgrounds the lack of adult-prescribed structure encourages social and moral growth.
2.  Adventure playgrounds provide for change and flexibility.
3.  Adventure playgrounds provide for fantasy making as opposed to fantasy feeding.
4.  Adventure playgrounds provide for physical and psychological development through self-selected risk taking.
5.  Adventure playgrounds provide for mainstreaming and integration of diverse groups.
6.  Adventure playgrounds are creative settings for the modeling of play behavior for children by adults.[23]

The English playground reformer Lady Allen of Hurtwood has, perhaps, most clearly summarized the significance of Adventure playgrounds, arguing that

> Adventure playgrounds are perhaps the most revolutionary experiment we know for absorbing the interest and releasing the energies of young people. Children the world over have a deep urge to experiment with earth, fire, water and timber. They need to be masters of the materials at hand and be free to move them around to suit their own desires and to create their own seeming chaos. They delight to work with real tools, to use them in their own way and at their own pace without criticism or censure.[24]

Fig. 2.9.   Emdrup provides space for ordinary childhood games such as ball play—cleverly contained in a limited space by wooden partitions. Note the word "PAX" (peace) on the wall—a clear expression of the social values developed through the nonformal education program of the playground. *Photograph by Robin Moore.*

Fig. 2.10.  View down the "main street" of Emdrup "children's village" lined with camps and clubhouses of previous generations of children, now in a woodland setting that has grown up over the years. *Photograph by Robin Moore.*

Fig. 2.11.   View across a well-maintained backyard of a beautifully detailed old clubhouse constructed by children years ago but still used by today's young inhabitants of the neighborhood. *Photograph by Robin Moore.*

Fig. 2.12.  View along the outer perimeter of the earth berm constructed originally to hide the messy children's adventure play environment from the residential neighborhood and now an attractive woodland slope covered with wildflowers—a natural asset in the community. *Photograph by Robin Moore.*

## Designer Playgrounds

During the early postwar period, playgrounds in the United States changed very little. Traditional designs established in the early part of the century were largely copied and repeated. It was not until the mid-1960s that the new concepts of playgrounds began to develop as a result of a larger urban reform movement.

In many respects, the new playgrounds that were developed beginning in the mid-1960s recalled themes developed by playground reformers during the progressive reform of the 1890s. Community advocates, including civic leaders, designers, educators and park and recreation professionals, attempted to provide play settings that would meet the needs of children and that would aesthetically complement the environments in which they were set.

The impetus for the development of designer playgrounds in the United States came out of the late 1960s and early 1970s. Architects such as M. Paul Friedberg developed a number of highly innovative parks and playgrounds in New York City. Perhaps the most well-known project undertaken by Friedberg was the playground for the Riis Houses located between 6th and 10th Streets along East River Drive (figs. 2.13 – 2.14). Wishing to create a "total play environment" for the children who used the playground, Friedberg explained how he and his associates "created experiences comparable to those a child might find elsewhere in widely scattered areas — a mountain, a tunnel, a tree house — and brought these together into a single environment. The experiences are separated not by fences but by changes in level and by other subtleties of design, the result is a series of architectonic forms that have an organic relationship."[25] Friedberg's playground at Riis represented a significant advance in playground design. Many of his designs emphasized the use of natural materials for the construction of benches and climbing apparatuses. The idea of "linked play" with children moving from one play area to another area was emphasized. While many of Friedberg's design innovations seem obvious today, they represented an important advance for the period (fig. 2.6).

Other designers from this period, such as Richard Dattner, developed innovative architectural designs employing water play and climbing forms. In

Fig. 2.13 and 2.14.   Jacob Riis playground in New York City, photographed in 1965 (M. Paul Friedberg, designer), one of the first attempts to move away from the traditional approach to playgrounds, using metal pipe equipment set in asphalt. In this case, the designer has used geometric, three-dimensional forms surfaced with recycled granite blocks to create a greater opportunity for climbing activity and chasing games such as hide-and-seek. *Photograph by Robin Moore.*

Fig. 2.14.

a design for a playground in Central Park, for example, Dattner included geometric cement forms that could be used for climbing and playing games such
as hide-and-seek as well as shallow wading pools and water sprays that could
be played in by children (fig. 2.7).[26]

**Conclusion**

The urban playgrounds developed by figures such as Friedberg and Dattner during the mid- and late-1960s represent a significant advance in playground design. Of greatest significance is that these and other designers from the period began to realize the potential of the playground to function as an environment—one which began to take advantage of natural as well as constructed forms. In chapter 3 we review current research on playground design and use and in chapter 4 return to some of the themes explored in this chapter by looking at a number of examples of contemporary playground design.

# 3

# PLAYGROUNDS

## THEORY AND RESEARCH

D espite the widespread use of playgrounds and their importance in the development of children, there is relatively little psychological, social, or curricular research on playgrounds. A search of the literature revealed the following areas of research: (1) gender differences on the playground, (2) choices of equipment and types of playgrounds, (3) motor activities of preschool children, (4) the playground as social center, (5) playground behaviors of exceptional children, (6) aggression in playground settings, and (7) attitudes about play. Research on safety is dealt with separately in chapter 6.

### Gender Differences on the Playground

Sex-role stereotyping and classifying certain playground activities as more appropriate for boys than for girls is an issue that received a great deal of attention during the late 1960s and early 1970s. Despite an increased awareness of the problem of gender discrimination, differences between boys and girls in their patterns of play and behavior on playgrounds remain widespread. The question arises whether these differences in behavior are based on the socialization of boys versus girls, or are they fundamentally biological or genetic? Although this question remains hotly debated in many different contexts, studies on playground behavior and interaction do not provide an answer. A

Fig. 3.1.   Exploring the possibilities of play on a timber jungle gym. *Photograph by Michael Carlebach.*

literature clearly articulates that boys engage in significantly different behaviors from girls in playground settings.

Janet Lever, in a 1976 study based on observations, interviews, questionnaires, and diaries examined the leisure activities of fifth-grade children. She found that of time not spent in school, 24 percent was spent in nonplay activities, 24 percent in vicarious pastimes (mostly watching television), and 52 percent in play. While looking at the organization of children's play activities, Lever found that the organization of their play activities differed significantly according to the gender of the children. She concluded that boys played more outdoors, in larger groups, included themselves in play activities involving a wider age range, participated in more competitive games, and played games that lasted longer than those of girls. Lever also found that girls more frequently played in boys' games than boys did in girls' games. She suggests that differences in leisure patterns lead to the development of different social skills and capacities.[1]

In 1981, Kathryn Borman, in a series of studies for the National Institute of Education, looked at the interpersonal relationships, playground games, and social cognitive skills of third through sixth graders. In the first study dealing with the ecology of children's play, a self-report of students revealed that game preferences depended on grade level and gender. Older boys participated more in complex and competitively structured team games than did younger children or girls.

Borman's second study was longitudinal and dealt with social development. In this study she found that cognitive skills, physical skills, and intellectual functioning were positively correlated with social behavioral ratings and game-playing status.

From findings of her third study, which dealt with negotiating playground games, she suggests that active involvement in games appears to contribute to cognitive development. Boys' games provide a richer environment for abstract concepts of power, roles, and rules than do the games played by girls. Boys spend more time negotiating and organizing and playing the game itself. Discussion of rules in games such as kickball tend to be far more complex than in hopscotch.[2]

Fig. 3.2. Testing oneself on a climbing apparatus. *Photograph by Michael Carlebach.*

Judith Lyons, in a study entitled "Sex Differences in Aggressive and Withdrawn Behavior on the Playground," videotaped and coded for social and aggressive behavior the playground activities of 117 fourth- and sixth-grade students in Canada. She found boys to be more physically aggressive and active than girls. Girls spent more time with peers outside the context of games than boys did.[3]

In a follow-up study to her 1981 research, Kathryn Borman with Lawrence Kurdek explored grade and gender differences in children's playground games. They found that grade and gender influenced the complexity of children's playground activities. Older children's play activities were more complex than those of younger children and the complexity of children's games increased significantly as the children matured over the one-year period. Boys were more likely than girls to participate in more complex activities, such as highly competitive team games. For boys, game complexity was positively related to understanding game rules and negatively related to interpersonal understanding, whereas for girls, game complexity was positively related to interpersonal understanding.[4]

Anthony Pelligrini and Jane Perlmutter, in a 1988 study entitled "Rough and Tumble Play on the Elementary School Playground," described rough and tumble play as including laughing, running, jumping, open-hand beating, wrestling, play fighting, chasing, and fleeing. They differentiated this type of play from aggressive behavior—including frowning, hitting, pushing, taking, and grabbing—which most often was brought on by property disputes. As one might expect, rough and tumble play occurred much more frequently on playgrounds with soft surfaces. Researchers suggested that rough and tumble play had educational and developmental value. Reciprocal role taking provided by rough and tumble play helped children develop social perspective–taking ability, especially boys.[5] In a follow-up study, Pelligrini found that rough and tumble play led children to play games with rules and was positively correlated for boys with measures of social competence.[6]

Pia Bjorklid, in a study of the frequency of outdoor play in open space play areas in two housing estates in Stockholm, found that boys were allowed out in the play areas more than girls at every age except birth to three years.

Young children and girls spent little time outdoors. Boys and girls between the ages of seven and twelve differed most in the amount of time spent outdoors.[7]

## Choices of Equipment and Types of Playgrounds

In a number of studies researchers have attempted to determine children's preferences for various types of playground equipment and designs. Joe Frost and E. Stickland, in a 1985 study entitled "Equipment Choices of Young Children During Free Play," provided children in kindergarten through second grade (n = 138) the choice of using three different playgrounds (*A*, *B*, and *C*). Playground *A* was a single structure with several activities for climbing and dramatic play and included swings, a slide, a fireman's pole, and a ladder. Playground *B* had sixteen structures designed for gross motor activity including balance beams, chinning bars, a slide, a jungle gym, and obstacle climbers. Playground *C* had a slide, a boat, a fort, a car, a storage area, a picnic table, climbers, wheeled vehicles, and used or found materials such as tires, spools, barrels, railroad ties, and utility poles. Playground *C* cost considerably less to build than the others and was chosen 63 percent of the time by the children. Playground *A* was the second most frequent choice made by the children. Younger children chose playground *C* more often than *A* or *B*. As grade level increased, *A* and *B* were chosen more frequently. Older children were more involved with games with rules. The children preferred complex structures that provided several play options and equipment that was moveable and could be used in different ways.[8]

Robin Moore asked boys and girls ages nine through twelve to draw all of their favorite places. Playgrounds were the second most frequent element in children's drawings. Particular pieces of equipment were often mentioned rather than the whole playground. Playgrounds in parks were very popular as were adventure playgrounds.[9]

Frost and Campbell compared the play choices of second-grade children on conventional and creative playgrounds. The dominant choices on both types of playgrounds were the moveable or action-oriented equipment. Chil-

Fig. 3.3.
Developing a
new perspective on things.
*Photograph by Michael Carlebach.*

Fig. 3.4.
A nontraditional slide being
used as a climbing apparatus.
*Photograph by Michael Carlebach.*

46

Fig. 3.5.
Head first.
*Photograph by Michael Carlebach.*

47

Fig. 3.6.
All things must come to an end.
*Photograph by Michael Carlebach.*

dren were more interested in equipment that supported complex play than they were in equipment that had only limited function.[10]

Campbell and Frost also compared the cognitive and social behaviors of second-grade children on traditional and creative playgrounds. They found more associative, cooperative, constructive, dramatic, and solitary play on the creative playground and more functional and parallel play on the traditional playground. They concluded that the type of play environment is related to types of play.[11]

Carl Gabbard and Elizabeth LeBlanc in their study, "Movement Activity Levels on Traditional and Contemporary Playground Structures," compared use of traditional and creative playground apparatus by kindergarten through fourth-grade children. Creative playground equipment (tires, metal tunnels, fire poles, ladders, and observation tower platforms) was consistently more popular than traditional equipment (slides and swings) with every age group.[12]

Craig Hart and Robert Sheehean in their study, "Preschoolers' Play Behavior in Outdoor Environments: Effects of Traditional and Contemporary Playgrounds," examined the effects of two different outdoor playground environments on the social, cognitive, and physical aspects of play behavior of preschool children. They defined contemporary playgrounds as having sculptural and organic forms, emphasizing novel shapes and textures configured in aesthetically pleasing formats. Although sculptured and organic forms may be aesthetically pleasing to adults, their fixed character may make them less conducive to active and imaginative play for children. The researchers found more sitting and standing behavior on the contemporary playground, and more climbing behavior on the traditional playground but no other significant differences. The researchers did not suggest that verbal interaction, cognitive play, or social play were influenced by either type of playground.[13]

Finally, Carl Gabbard, in a 1979 study on playground apparatus and children's muscular endurance, provided different types of play apparatus to two groups of four- to six-year-olds. The purpose of the study was to test the effects of specific play equipment on upper body muscular endurance. Children who used the play environment that had overhead climbers and ladders

Fig. 3.7. Free play with "qualifications." *Photograph by Michael Carlebach.*

had significantly increased musuclar endurance. Gabbard concluded that experience provided by a well-equipped playground can contribute to increased upper body muscular efficiency of young children.[14]

A limitation of nearly all these studies is the limited range of play settings available to the children in each playground site under investigation. None of the studies, for instance, included children's interactions with more manipulative settings such as sand, water, dirt, and vegetation.

## Motor Activities of Preschool Children

The use of children's motor skills on the playground suggests that playground activities contribute in important ways to the development of fine and gross motor skills. Rita Yerkes, in a 1982 study entitled "A Playground That Extends the Classroom," found that playground participation in an adventure playground setting helped children improve their visual-motor integration skills. Children who used the creative-adventure playground also became more assertive and imaginative than the children who did not have the playground experience. Yerkes concluded that creative-adventure playgrounds can be used to reinforce fundamental learning tasks because they capitalize on children's natural exploratory tendencies.[15]

According to Catherine Poest, Jean Williams, David Witt and Mary Atwood in their study, "Physical Activity Patterns of Preschool Children," children need to have regular, vigorous physical activity. They determined that even active children rarely exercised vigorously enough to benefit their hearts. Fitness and motor skills that needed to be developed were best provided by instructional classes rather than free-play activities. The amount of physical activity children were involved in was clearly seasonal. Boys were consistently more active than girls on the playground, and nursery school children were more active than day-care children. Nursery school teachers tended to be better educated about children's developmental needs than were day-care personnel and, in turn, were more aware of the need for children to participate in physical activities.[16]

Fig. 3.8. The challenge of a climbing net. *Photograph by Michael Carlebach.*

## The Playground as Social Center

Except in the historical literature from the beginning of this century, there is little discussion of the playground as a social center in the playground research. Alasdair Roberts in his 1978 article, "Extraversion and Outdoor Play in Middle Childhood," concluded that daily exposure to school playgrounds seems to be the most important factor in children's knowledge of traditional games, rather than personality or out of school habits. He suggests that the school playground plays a critical role as a social center for the development of middle school children.[17]

Moighan-Nourot, Scales, and Van Hoorn used various ethnographic methods to look at play as it occurred in the playground setting. As he undertook the research, Scales identified specific expected developmental outcomes that would result from playground activities, including self-achievement and mastery, learning through imitating adults, affective development through fantasy, and sociolinguistic and verbal development through interaction. The development of social competence was the central subject of the study. Researchers focused particular attention on three different settings, including a sand table, a large sand pit, and a large climber, and the effect they had on the socialization process of the children being studied. They suggest that interaction often depends on features of the setting and that children use their imaginations to integrate their play into various settings or to modify the setting to fit their needs.[18]

## Playground Behaviors of Exceptional Children

Mogford reviewed the research on the play of exceptional children in a chapter of a book published in 1977.[19] From findings of the studies cited he suggests that mere provision of appropriate playthings is not enough to foster exploration and play in severely handicapped children but that social interaction and attention is necessary. In a series of studies, researchers established that mentally retarded children do play in environments that provide encouragement for

Fig. 3.9. An "uplifting" experience. *Photograph by Michael Carlebach.*

them. A comparison of the play of mentally handicapped and normal children determined that they differed most markedly in their choices of play materials. The mentally handicapped children chose more structured and less-creative playthings than did normal children.[20] A link may exist between language and speech problems and children's imaginative play although the exact relationship is not clear.[21] Sound is particularly satisfying to blind children at play. Because exploration is inhibited, blind children need a lot of encouragement and support. The imitative play of these children is limited to imitation of sound.[22]

A study of the play activities of mentally retarded children was reported by Daniel Donder and John Nietupski in their 1981 article, "Nonhandicapped Adolescents Teaching Playground Skills to Their Mentally Retarded Peers." Nonhandicapped middle school students taught age-appropriate playground recreation skills to three students in a class for the moderately retarded. The retarded students' percentage of appropriate playground behavior and contact with nonhandicapped students increased.[23]

## Aggression in Playground Settings

In a 1974 study, Bellak and Antell compared the aggression of adults toward children and children toward each other in Germany, Italy, and Denmark. A significant relationship was found between the level of aggression manifested by parents and the aggressive behavior of children as they participated in playground activities.[24]

Murphy, Hutchinson, and Bailey in a 1983 study entitled "Behavioral School Psychology Goes Outdoors: The Effect of Organized Games on Playground Aggression," looked at the effectiveness of providing organized games on the aggressive behaviors of 344 kindergarten through second grade children. Games, rope jumping, and foot racing, along with an infrequently used time-out procedure significantly reduced the frequency of aggressive playground behaviors.[25]

## Attitudes about Play

As in other areas of playground research, studies of attitudes about play are limited. In a study by Rothlein and Brett, parents and teachers of two to six year olds completed questionnaires on their perceptions of the function and value of play. Parents saw play only as fun or amusement. Although teachers recognized play as an opportunity for social and cognitive development, they did not view play as an integral part of the curriculum. Parents did not support having children spend a large part of their preschool time in play, despite the fact that children, their parents, and their teachers all identified outdoor play, together with dramatic play, blocks, and art activities, as being their favorite pastime.[26]

## Conclusion

Although playgrounds have an important role to play in the educational system —and are a significant component of almost every early childhood and elementary school — understanding of them based on current research is still extremely limited. As noted in this chapter, researchers have only just begun to explore the role of gender in children's behavior in playspaces, why children choose certain types of play settings over others, how playgrounds can contribute to the various areas of child development, the role of playgrounds as centers for social development, the potential of playgrounds to help children with special needs, the problems posed by aggressive behavior on the playground, and, finally, what types of play activities are valued most by children.

We believe that the greatest need for research is to advance understanding of the role that playgrounds can play in the developmental process of children. How important is it, for example, for children to participate in certain types of play activity, not just for their physical development and well-being but also for their intellectual and social development? Carefully controlled studies are needed to document the benefits that may be derived from particular types of settings or programs. Can children with special needs be served by activities associated with playgrounds in ways that are not possible in other educational settings? Are certain types of playgrounds, such as adventure playgrounds, of particular importance to children whose opportunities for development are limited by poverty or parental neglect? Do the cognitively rich environments created by such playground settings contribute significantly to overall child development?

Such research has inherent problems because many of the questions that need to be addressed are interdisciplinary. As a result, playground research must involve the collaboration of individuals in fields as diverse as psychology, architecture, early childhood and elementary education, exercise environmental design, and special education. There is even a role to be played by individuals from disciplines such as sociology and history.

From the current research on playgrounds one clearly sees the enormous potential they could have in shaping and positively influencing the social, psychological, intellectual, and physical development of children. In subsequent chapters, we suggest ways in which playground potential could be maximized to enhance the development and enjoyment of all children.

# 4

# INNOVATIVE PLAYGROUNDS

## AN INTERNATIONAL SURVEY

We discuss next existing playgrounds and how they might develop in the future. We define playgrounds in this chapter as any place organized by adults for children's play. This description may seem overly broad and lead the discussion into areas far removed from conventional notions of playgrounds. An enormous variety of organized provisions for children's play exists in the world today, however, and our role here is to introduce them to the reader, describe the primary characteristics that distinguish them from other forms, and provide sufficient material to carry the concepts forward into new applications.

The world is changing socially, culturally, and environmentally at an ever-increasing, some would say alarming, rate. In cities such as New York, many parents no longer allow their children out in streets that until recently were children's traditional roaming ground and the de facto real playground of the city.[1] The city has lost its innocence. Streets (and traditional playgrounds) have become the violent terrain of drug dealers and gang warfare. The only option for many children is to stay indoors with TV, a primary playmate that delivers even more violent fare. Under these circumstances, children desperately need a safe, stimulating haven where they can interact with peers and exercise their minds, bodies, and spirits under the guidance of caring adults.

Social circumstances in smaller cities are nowhere as extreme as those in New York City; nonetheless, the social threats toward children and the

Fig. 4.1. A playleader works with immigrant Algerian children in a manipulative indoor environment, encouraging them to explore, to "play with" aspects of daily life, thereby helping them to integrate aspects of their two cultures, Arabic and French. *Photograph by D. Revault.*

traffic danger (the primary killer of children outside the home) mean that children's free-play range away from home is more and more restricted as parental apprehension increases.

Changes in family composition and work habits since the 1950s have also influenced the development of innovative playgrounds, especially in Europe. Families are small. In some northern European countries population growth is hovering around zero. Older siblings are no longer available to look after younger brothers and sisters. Families with both parents working and single parent families have become firmly established social characteristics. The long history of concern for children's welfare after school and during the summer months has, over the years, resulted in a broad array of social institutions. These have evolved not simply as custodial arrangements but as centers of creative activity, the best of which view playing and learning as an integrated process covering all aspects of child and community development. Adventure playgrounds, play parks, toy libraries, urban farms, children's farms, play busses, open playgrounds, and animated play events, have become a vital force in the development of local culture.

These innovative facilities and programs all fall within the realm of nonformal education. They are viewed as both extensions and complements to the formal educational, schoolbased experience of the child.

The most common characteristics innovative programs and facilities share is a playful spirit and attitude by adult staff who recognize that play is children's primary motivation to engage with each other and their surroundings. The specially trained staff are called playleaders, social pedagogs, animators, or playworkers, depending on the country and the particular background of its play professions.[2] The field is most developed in the Nordic countries where the social pedagogy profession has standing and training procedures equivalent to those of teachers in the formal education system. Social pedagogs, as the name implies, "teach" or facilitate creative activity in the nonformal social sector of cultural and community development in youth clubs, community social centers, summer camps, and all manner of recreation programs. The terms *playleader* and *playworker* are synonymous and are the most commonly used terms in many English-speaking countries where the

Fig. 4.2.
Through effective
playleadership, traditionally
structured playgrounds can
be transformed into a multitude of
settings for creative open-ended play.
*Photograph by Robin Moore.*

field has developed to varying degrees. It is most advanced in the United Kingdom although there has been resistence to achieving the Nordic level of professional institutionalization. Animation is a term used in many French- and Spanish-speaking countries. The concept has a somewhat different orientation in these cultures toward a more explicitly defined cultural frame of reference. "Animators use play as a tool, to change behavior, perceptions, and attitudes . . . using the movement, life, and vigor of play to achieve social purposes, to create situations . . . helping children express, apply, and assimilate experience in personal and community life."[3]

The existence of professional play staff is a crucial dimension of every facility, and the expertise of such staff will account for the popularity of any particular facility and the degree to which it is a vital force in the development of local culture (fig. 4.1). To appreciate the great variety of places organized by adults for children's play, it is necessary to expand one's vision beyond existing stereotypes, not necessarily to abandon them, for each has continuing validity in particular local circumstances, even the much vilified, so-called traditional playground (fig. 4.2).


### Adventure Playgrounds

It is important to point out that the adventure playground concept that took shape in Emdrup is still arguably the most significant playground innovation. It is also the most challenging to implement, which explains why, fifty years later, adventure playgrounds have still not caught on in most countries (including the United States). The very best examples are still to be found in Copenhagen, their birthplace. Bispevangens is a large adventure playground, founded in 1965, located in the Copenhagen district of Ballerup. The site, situated on a broad strip of land between high-rise housing blocks and a subway line, was designed as an adventure playground from the beginning with high grassy berms that enclose the whole area (fig. 4.3). At the far end of the site is a large circular area devoted to the traditional adventure playground activity of children building their own community of huts from scrap lumber. In the

Fig. 4.3.  Bispevangens, a large adventure playground in the Copenhagen district of Ballerup, is surrounded by a continuous grass-covered berm that provides the occupants with a strong sense of enclosure and protection from the outside world. The playground is a special place where special things can happen. The berm also keeps the unsightly results of children's play from the sensitive eyes of neighbors. *Photograph by Robin Moore.*

Fig. 4.4.  Animals are a normal feature of adventure playgrounds. *Photograph by Robin Moore.*

Fig. 4.5. Small planted areas looked after by the children add a sense of personalization and caring for the environment. *Photograph by Robin Moore.*

center of the space is a huge firepit almost constantly in service. Children are quietly working on their buildings, making repairs, improving the interiors with scraps of material brought from home, adding to the gaily painted exteriors. Any visitor will constantly be invited into one or another hut by its proud builders.

Animals are all over the playground (fig. 4.4). A sheep is temporarily tethered to one of the play structures. On top of the grass berm, two girls are playing with a donkey, petting it, taking rides around the berm looking down on their domain.

Several children are in the covered rabbit hutch area looking after their charges (according to their "contract," if they want a rabbit they must be responsible for its care). Each of the about thirty hutches is personalized with painted decorations of many different species. A nine-year-old girl is cradling a beautiful specimen with a black, shiny coat. It seems almost as big as she is. There is a pig pen and a duck pond. Chickens wander everywhere. A child has just checked the nesting boxes and walks by with a plump brown egg in each hand.

Small gardens and planted areas have been introduced throughout the space, reinforcing a sense of an informal but caring environment (fig. 4.5). Near the entrance to the site is a community building that houses a children's center, a small library, community meeting rooms, a café where older members of the community gather to gossip, and a club for adolescents completely managed by young people.

Near the entrance also is a workshop building where children can check out tools and equipment to work with. Nearby, a playleader is helping a young girl learn to use a saw to cut some wood for a project. Another playleader is assisting a group of children with a cooking activity. They are making traditional flour-and-water dough. Some children are rolling out strips and twisting it around the end of a thin stick to roast it over an open fire. Others are patting it out into flatbread loaves to be cooked on a metal grid over the hot coals (fig. 4.6). This simple pleasure is still a delight for these children, even though they live in one of the most industrially advanced countries in the world. No one is exactly telling the children to do these things. They are motivated by the hands-on opportunity to create something that smells and tastes good. The fine muscle coordination, social interaction, sensory discrimination, sense of autonomy, and growth of self-esteem seem to evolve before one's eyes.

Fig. 4.6.
Children delight in
the creative transformations
of cooking. A simple flatbread
dough is all that is required.
Children living in even the most
sophisticated industrial culture
take pleasure in simple activities.
*Photograph by Robin Moore.*

Fig. 4.7. The Bispevangens stage provides a setting for all kinds of outdoor community performances. *Photograph by Robin Moore.*

Fig. 4.8.   Legally blind children guide each other around the pathways of the Lady Allen Playground for Children with Special Needs, London, England, run by the Handicapped Adventure Playground Association (HAPA), founded by Lady Allen of Hurtwood. *Photography by Robin Moore.*

Bispevangens has been operating long enough that the children of its original children now play there. In fact, it will not be long before grandchildren begin to show up. The place is a self-evidently and extraordinarily valuable social asset in the community, not just a "safe haven" but a creative, multifaceted cultural facility focused on children's needs but related to the whole community. The playground has its own brass band. In a stage and performance area all manner of community, musical, and dramatic events are presented (fig. 4.7).

In this highly developed form, adventure playgrounds have not spread extensively beyond Denmark, except to the United Kingdom where the idea was imported directly from Emdrup in the late 1940s. But they have been difficult to sustain and the quality has been variable, primarily because of the limited opportunities for play leadership training (only two programs in the whole country) compared to the highly developed social pedagogy profession in Denmark.

### Adventure Playgrounds for Children with Special Needs

In the late 1960s, Lady Allen of Hurtwood, who had helped import the original adventure playground idea to England, turned her attention to the needs of children with disabilities and established the first adventure playground for the handicapped (as it was called originally) in Chelsea in the protected grounds of a large vicarage. Over the years, the movement has grown to five sites in the London area. The basic concept remains the same: to provide the means for children to plan and create their own community, in this case adapted to the circumstances of children with special needs (figs. 4.8, 4.9).

In a later development, reflecting a move toward the integration of children with disabilities into the general community, the concept of the "playground for all children" was developed, the idea being to provide a play area "open to children of all abilities and disabilities" and accessible to all. An early example was the Playground for All Children in Queens, New York, a project that was founded to commemorate the International Year of the Child (1979). Begining in 1987, the International Association for the Child's Right to Play (IPA) in Sweden developed an accessible playground for all children in Vaxholm, just outside Stockholm. The idea is slowly spreading around the world with examples in places such as Bombay, India; Hong Kong; and Vancouver, British Columbia. Flood Park, San Mateo, California, is an example of how an accessible play area can be integrated into a large community park (figs. 4.10, 4.11, 4.12).

Fig. 4.9.   Provision of low-cost outdoor musical instruments are emphasized on the HAPA playgrounds. *Photograph by Robin Moore.*

Fig. 4.10.   Welcoming tower structure with wind chimes marks the entrance to Flood Park accessible playground, California. *Photograph by MIG, Inc.*

Fig. 4.11.   Flood Park playground provides accessible features to people of all ages.
*Photograph by MIG, Inc.*

Fig. 4.12. Accessible water play is a special feature of the Flood Park playground. *Photograph by MIG, Inc.*

Fig. 4.13.   A pottery kiln built by children in a Stockholm Playpark. *Photograph by Jan Duroj.*

Fig. 4.14.   Parents and children playing together on a simple play structure at Hanegi Playpark, Tokyo. *Photograph by Robin Moore.*

Fig. 4.15.   A playleader and children making traditional Japanese toys from bamboo in Hanegi Playpark, Tokyo. *Photograph by Robin Moore.*

## Playparks

In response to increasing motorized traffic in the streets and diminishing informal open spaces in the city, playgrounds with trained leaders began in nine parks in Stockholm in June 1937. Known as playparks, the concept was pioneered by Stina Wretlind-Larsson, a physical education teacher and social worker. She was one of the playleaders for the three summer months and the following year was appointed superintendent for the system of fifteen. At its peak in the early 1980s, there were 210 units in the system, including between forty and fifty school-based sites, twenty to thirty seasonal playgrounds, and several mobile facilities. More recently, a "play recession" in Sweden has dramatically cut the scope of the program down to approximately eighty permanent sites. The playpark idea was very simple: to establish in a corner of each public park in the city a facility focused on children's play and staffed by trained leaders (fig. 4.13). Over the years this idea was nurtured by Frited Stockholm (Stockholm Leisure Department) and grew into an internationally renowned program that eventually spread to England (again), especially London, and also to Japan where the Hanegi Playpark, Setagaya Ward, Tokyo, was founded in the 1970s (figs. 4.14, 4.15).

In addition to the park itself and trained leadership, a key component of a playpark is a building that typically contains a multipurpose games and meeting room, crafts workshop, kitchen and café, lots of storage, and, perhaps, a space that adolescents can call their own. In front might be a terrace or deck for general hanging out. Although there may be fixed play structures such as swings, slides, and climbing structures, an equally strong focus is on temporary environments that are created by children according to seasonal cycles, availability of resources, fashions and trends in the prevailing childhood culture.

Orrleken Playpark, Karlstad, Sweden, is a playpark on an extensive site located on the shores of a large lake (fig. 4.16). Water play, therefore, has become a natural theme. The designers of this park were very clever in using the gentle topography sloping down to the shore. Water is pumped up to the top of the hill where it is available for play before running back down in a shallow

Fig. 4.16.   The inviting entrance to Orrleken Playpark, Karlstad, Sweden. *Photograph by Robin Moore.*

channel formed in a wide band of sloping asphalted circulation space (figs. 4.17, 4.18). At the top of the hill children had rigged out of scrap lumber their own Rube Goldberg water play contraption comprising a series of channels, troughs, and falls. With this mechanism, children amused themselves for hours redirecting the flows of water, floating sticks, leaves, and small flowers down the channels. By varying the amount of water going through the system they were able to conduct their own cause-and-effect experiments. As the water ran downhill the children dammed it to create miniature overflows, dam bursts, and "floods."

On another asphalted section of the hill, a "soapbox derby" was underway using vehicles that the children had constructed in the well-equipped shop in the park building (fig. 4.19). One of the playleaders had a stop watch and was timing each of the two-child teams (driver and pusher). The rest of the children were the cheering section. It was great fun (fig. 4.20).

The possibilities for wheeled toy play were extensive, supported by undulating asphalt surfaces and pathways bordered by vegetation and crossed by bridges, giving the feeling of a miniature highway (fig. 4.21). In another area was a large sand-covered area for swings (fig. 4.22). Although a small adventure playground section was also included, it was not the dominant feature. It is interesting to note that a number of children with various disabilities were present playing with the able-bodied children—an excellent example of genuine integration. One of the playleaders said he had been working there many years and talked about how he loved the work. Of course, without this kind of committed, trained leadership this type of play facility would be completely unfeasible.

Fig. 4.17 and 4.18.   A temporary child/playleader-constructed hilltop water-play feature at Orrleken Playpark. *Photograph by Robin Moore.*

Fig. 4.18.

Fig. 4.19. A well-equipped workshop at Orrleken Playpark, where young people can work on a variety of play projects—constructing wheeled toys, for example. *Photograph by Robin Moore.*

Fig. 4.20.   A "Soapbox Derby" with trollies made by the children at Orrleken Playpark.
*Photograph by Robin Moore.*

Fig. 4.21.   A system of undulating pathways bordered by vegetation at Orrleken Play-park provides a complex exploratory environment, stimulating to the senses. *Photograph by Robin Moore.*

Fig. 4.22.   Huge, safe, sand-covered swings area surrounded by vegetative screens that also serve as a community "hangout" at Orrleken Playpark. *Photograph by Robin Moore.*

Fig. 4.23.   A small playbus in Munich, Germany, making a visit to a city park. *Photograph by Robin Moore.*

## Mobile Play Unit/Play Busses

There are many excellent examples of mobile play facilities. The concept is obvious: if children cannot get to the playground because it is too far away or simply nonexistent, take the playground to the children. Orrleken Playpark had a mobile play unit that made visits to neighborhoods in the city that lacked good play facilities.

The double-decker buses used as standard transportation vehicles in England began to be recycled early in the playbus, or mobile projects, movements. There are now dozens of playbuses in operation throughout the country under the umbrella of the National Playbus Association Mobile Projects Unit. Indeed, mobile programs have become so popular that the concept has been applied to a wide range of community education and commercial ventures that are far removed from children's play.

Undoubtedly, the most concentrated and comprehensive citywide playbus program is operated by Pedagogical Action in cooperation with the city of Munich, Bavaria. The fleet of seventeen vehicles covers a broad range of functions. The smallest is a van that circulates around the city parks with basic play equipment for young children (figs. 4.23, 4.24). A standard city bus has been converted into a computer playbus, staffed by high school student volunteer "computer nuts" and containing all manner of hands-on computer play which is very attractive to many children (fig. 4.25). The program is very playful and open-ended to keep it quite different from any feeling of school.

Another converted city bus has become a roving research lab that moves around the city carrying a group of young people who evaluate the parks, playgrounds, and other recreation sites. One of the most unique vehicles is a waterplaymobile that used to be a city fire engine (figs. 4.26, 4.27). Now it appears in the city neighborhoods not to put out fires but to offer all manner of waterplay opportunities. Normally, it uses parks where a slope is available because water runs downhill. Waterslides are set up using long sheets of polyethylene with water running down to lubricate them. A collection of plastic tubes, troughs, and dishes can be joined together to create water channels. Then of course there are sprays and playpools with model boats. The

Fig. 4.24.  Playbus contents provide neighborhood children with a diversity of play opportunities. *Photograph by Robin Moore.*

accent is on pure fun! Nothing finer on a hot summer day. An Austrian playbus travels to parks containing lakes where children can use materials and tools to build rafts then try them out and engage in various adventures.

One of the oldest of Pedagogical Action's playbuses is a large truck called the "Pumpernikel Cirkus." Vividly decorated like a circus vehicle, it travels around making stopovers of several days in the neighborhoods of the city (fig. 4.28). It also shows up at special events in the city. Children can come and create a circus together. Assisted by the animators they learn circus skills such as trapeze techniques and balancing tricks, develop dramatic shows, and make up their own versions of traditional acts such as the "lady being sawed in half." Once the show is finally ready, a performance is put on for family and friends. It is a chance for children to learn real skills and to work together to achieve a collective result.

The Music Playbus has a similar developmental impact but through the creation of communal music using a wide range of percussion instruments. The possibilities are endless. Art playbuses give children in low-income areas opportunities for self-expression in the visual arts. Inter-Action, a British organization, developed a Media Bus that enabled young people to make video programs on local issues and events, which could later be aired on the community access channel. Again, this concept has yet to develop in the United States, even though it is particularly appropriate for low-density and/or low-income communities where young people cannot get access to creative play programs. Every community contains spaces such as parking lots, plazas, and streets that can be converted into temporary playgrounds for a few days when the playbus comes by.

Fig. 4.25.   A computer playbus, Munich, Germany. *Photograph by Robin Moore.*

Fig. 4.26.   A water playbus made from an old fire truck. *Photograph by Robin Moore.*

Fig. 4.27.
A simple waterslide
extending down a grassy
slope from the water playbus.
*Photograph by Robin Moore.*

Fig. 4.28.   Karussel, the circus playbus where children produce their own circus programs. *Photograph by Robin Moore.*

Fig. 4.29, 4.30, and 4.31. Days of Play, a four-day play event for the whole family in Munich, Germany, including crafts with traditional indigenous materials, adventure play, playbusses converted from traditional workers' shelters, and play "on air" in pneumatic equipment. *Photographs by Robin Moore.*

## Temporary Playgrounds/Play Events

In Germany, Pedagogical Action and Inter-Action, in England, two community arts and animation organizations, have pioneered the concept of play events that transform public spaces into temporary playgrounds for a short time, anywhere from one day to two to several weeks.

Days of Play, a four-day biennial event held in the Olympic Park, Munich, is part of a ten-day play festival held at sites all over the city. The huge central activity space, overlooking a large lake, was literally transformed into a playful city with the offerings of Pedagogical Action and numerous other animation groups from German-speaking Europe (Austria, Switzerland, as well as Hungary and Poland). The event attracts thousands of families from all over the city, and apart from anything else, it is a fantastic promotional event for PLAY!—for "children of all ages" (figs. 4.29, 4.30, 4.31).

Mini-Munich, another type of temporary play event developed by Pedagogical Action, is held in a huge indoor sports hall at the same Olympic Park over a six-week summer period, with two thousand children participating in building a miniature version of the real Munich (figs. 4.32, 4.33).

Playful City, a weekend event developed as part of their version of the arts festival programs in cities in North Carolina, is inspired in part by Mini-Munich and the adventure playground concept. In a city park, a large supply of stimulating and attractive "scrap" material is made available to the general public, to anyone who wants to participate in building a "playful city," in other words, whatever imaginations can create constrained only by the limitations of the materials (fig. 4.34). Because it is a weekend activity, held within an arts festival, it presents an ideal opportunity for parents and children to play together. Because of the open feeling of free creativity, adolescents are attracted to participate and make their own statements. One high school group of friends from the crosscountry running team made a "Monument to Clean Air," for example (fig. 4.35).

Fig. 4.30.

Fig. 4.31.

Fig. 4.32. A street in Mini-Munich—always something going on among the children.
*Photograph by Wolfgang Zacharias.*

Fig. 4.33. The Employment Exchange in Mini-Munich — an important place in the city. With luck, one can get jobs to earn money. The cards show vacant jobs, for instance, tailor, taxi driver, car mechanic, artist, gardener, trash collector, waiter, professor. Sometimes there is a lot of unemployment and long lines form in front of the Employment Exchange. *Photograph by Wolfgang Zacharias.*

Fig. 4.34. Playful City workshop, using scrap materials to attract the whole family into an adventure play setting in Raleigh, North Carolina. *Photograph by PLAE, Inc.*

## Play Streets

Recognition of the fact that in most urban neighborhoods the street is the de facto playground for most children has prompted the concept of the Play Street in many communities over the years. Minimum interventions have included posting signs saying "Play Street" and devices that regulate the amount and speed of vehicular traffic. Although limited, such efforts are certainly better than none at all. The danger is that they can give children a false sense of security because in reality the traffic protection is minimal.

To address this issue, beginning in the early seventies, the Dutch developed a far more elaborate concept called the *Woonerf*, or "protected precinct," that involves a carefully delineated community planning procedure and set of technical standards for substantially changing the configurations of neighborhood streets in favor of pedestrians (figs. 4.36, 4.37, 4.38). In the intervening years the concept has spread to many European countries. Although not exclusively focused on the play needs of children, they are, in fact, the major beneficiaries. A major accomplishment of the Woonerf concept has been to return to children their natural habitat, to enable them to recapture their participation in a richer street-based community life.

Fig. 4.35.   High school students construct a "Monument to Clean Air" as their contribution to a Playful City. *Photograph by PLAE, Inc.*

Fig. 4.36.
Children play on the sidewalk,
protected in part by the
*Woonerf* principle.
*Photograph by Robin Moore.*

105

Fig. 4.37 and 4.38.   *Woonerfs* can make a dramatic change to the ambience of city neighborhood streets, making them far more attractive to children and adults alike. *Photograph by Robin Moore.*

106

Fig. 4.38.

Fig. 4.39.   Caring for ponies and pony riding are important activities of Dutch Children's Farms and the Youth Farms in Germany. *Photograph by Robin Moore.*

## Urban/Children's Farms

The Dutch, British, and Germans have been the leaders of a movement for several decades to bring some aspects of rural life styles and environment into the hands of urban children, who, the joke goes, think milk comes from a carton rather than a cow. Although the style and content of these types of facilities vary between countries and even in the same country, the underlying intention is to provide a vehicle for children to get close to natural processes. In some cases the approach is more didactic, in others more playful. In all cases, the approach offers a nonformal intervention into the educational and recreational life of the community through which dimensions of work that children enjoy immensely and play are combined. The Children's Garden Service in The Hague, the Netherlands, provides large areas where school groups can cultivate garden plots to grow flowers and vegetables. The result is a huge field of blazing color. Gardens are often combined with transposed elements of the farm experience where (as in Danish adventure playgrounds) children can experience and work with animals ranging from rabbits to horses. A children's farm can provide a wonderful kind of club for children across a wide age range who all work together. In Rotterdam, the educational authorities have appointed a group of "school biologists" who work "at large" in the children's farms and schools (but are not attached to any particular school). Their job is to help, advise, facilitate, and stimulate interaction between children and nature. In essence, they are a special kind of "nature playleader."

In Germany, the Youth Farms are more play oriented. Many exist in suburban locations around Stuttgart. They are places where children can come during weekends and the summer months to relax and have creative fun in natural surroundings. Caring for horses and horse riding are important features, as in the Dutch Children's Farms (fig. 4.39). So is social development. The young people must take responsibility for running the facility as much as possible. Thus, the playground is a vehicle for democratic education.

An interesting adaptation of the children's farm concept is taking place in Japan. The Maioka project in Yokohama is focused on the conservation of old rice fields that form a series of terraces stepping down one of the nar-

Fig. 4.40, 4.41, and 4.42.   Maioka Yato Park—an "agri-culture park in an urban natural place" is located in the valley that is the source of the Maioka River above Yokohama. The park is run by a citizens' group, the Maioka Water and Greenery Society, whose aim is "introducing more nature into our daily lives." Photographs show planting rice (4.40), harvesting rice (4.41), and winter celebration in front of a replica of a stone-age house made from rice stems (4.42). *Photographs by Maioka Water and Greenery Society.*

row valleys presently on the fringe of the city but threatened with urban development. To plant rice, children bare their legs and wade in mud halfway up to their knees (figs. 4.40, 4.41, 4.42). It is difficult to think of a more sensory, playful experience for children. In the Maioka rice fields people of all ages can enjoy an activity that is central to Japanese culture. It is also an opportunity

Fig. 4.41.

for informal social contact in a very different setting from the traditionally formal occasions of much Japanese life. Especially at harvest time everyone can participate in the work and rituals of harvesting, making rice cakes, constructing rice-straw dolls, and so forth.

British urban farms have a similar child-and-community orientation. They also have a tradition of involvement by community artists who add a further creative dimension to the "farming" activities partly because the movement was started by Inter-Action, which is primarily a community arts organization.

An urban farm in Birmingham, England, is an excellent example of a diverse, community based facility (fig. 4.43). Entry from the street leads into

Fig. 4.42.

a hard-paved area that feels like a small farmyard. A group of children are there chatting with one of the leaders who looks young enough to still be in high school. A duck pond is the main feature. A greenhouse, hen house, and farm shed, housing office and workshop, border the edges of the space. Several ducks and chickens animate the space. A path leads out of the yard to a garden plot area on one side and a donkey paddock on the other. Across the quiet residential street from the main yard is an intimate, highly developed, gardenlike setting with a great profusion of different types of plants, vines climbing the walls, flowering shrubs, fruit and nut trees. A bee hive is located in one corner. Other areas are subtly subdivided by low fences. Interspersed among the living components are large display boards made by children to explain what goes on in this magic playing and learning garden. Bold drawings and short descriptions present the results of the children's investigations. The place is a crossroads between play and education yet is genuinely childlike, close to the feeling evoked in some of the best children's literature.

There is a strong atmosphere of caring and sensitive management. The space is tidy but not manicured, a rare example of ordered complexity that can come only from collective understanding that results from a continuous and open working relationship between a group of people—in this case, dozens of schoolchildren, their classroom teachers, and the trained farm staff.

The Farm in San Francisco has a similar feeling. One of the few urban farms in the United States, the Farm was founded by community artist Bonnie Sherk in an old warehouse building beside a highway exit. It features indoor community meeting and performance spaces, gardens, and animal husbandry spaces. This provides a setting for many imaginative community play events, for instance a "Hybernation Festival" (fig. 4.44).

### Open Playgrounds

The Open Playground is located in the Freizeitpark (leisure park) in Düsseldorf-Heerdt. Started in 1972 by a *bürgerinitiative* (an initiating group of the people), it is the finest example known to the authors of a playground created as a continuous experiment in democratic community decision making. The playground was built by the local community on Saturdays between 1972 and 1982 led by Klaus Spitzer, a high school art teacher. Over the years, the space continuously evolved according to the needs expressed by the community.

The design is primarily and specifically oriented toward the play requirements of the children. Economics, ease of maintenance, and aesthetics remain important secondary considerations. The participation of children and the observations of the way they play—on a site that is both a construction site and a playground—helps to ensure that the design is appropriate for the children. Age groups are not isolated from one another but "disentangled" by appropriate play facilities and other social settings, (fig. 4.45).

Fig. 4.43. An urban farm in Birmingham, England. Intimate, child-oriented nonformal education setting with a strong environmental program conducted by high school students. *Photograph by Robin Moore.*

Fig. 4.44. "Hybernation Festival" at the Farm, San Francisco, USA. *Photograph by Robin Moore.*

Fig. 4.45.   Relaxed community setting at the Open Playground, Dusseldorf, Germany. *Photograph by Klaus Spitzer.*

The independence of the community group provides a creative atmosphere, which reinforces a playful attitude about the "work." Action takes place through spontaneity and intuition. Because decisions are taken on the site, the group can make optimum use of the existing unique situation (*genus loci*) or take account of previously constructed or natural features, responding to them and integrating them into the continuing design process (the "dialectic of design"). This collective creative way of working has produced a great variety of structures, relief, plants, and materials that could not have been planned in advance. They address all of the senses (fig. 4.46). This process does not result in the one-sided definable style expected with the artistic expression of a single individual. The "style" is the variety; its attraction is its complexity.

The spatial treatment is based on "centers" and not on boundaries between areas. In this way numerous cell-like spaces arise that flow into one another. In the peripheral zones gray areas develop with spontaneous vegetation, reserves for subsequent expansion or informal adventure play areas.

The plants create play spaces and, above all, serve the purpose of play themselves. They have to be fast growing and robust. They are planted much more densely than normal although planned pathways are left open. Wild plants, ornamental species, and food plants are used equally (fig. 4.47).

The participation of children and young people and the help of a great number of local residents creates a broadly based and intense level of identification on the part of the users. Because the construction site was available for play from the very beginning, it exists at the same time as a constantly changing playground, that is always interesting, stimulating, and full of adventure. The boundaries between play and work are no longer sharply defined.

### Environmental Yards

A close companion to the Open Playground is the environmental yard concept that was developed at an elementary school in Berkeley, California, during the 1970s (figs. 4.48, 4.49, 4.50, 4.51).[4] The idea was to transform a typical asphalted urban schoolyard into a democratic learning and playing space by engaging the children, parents, teaching staff, and surrounding community in the transformation process. (fig. 4.52).

Fig. 4.46.
In the Open Playground,
vegetation is used to
stimulate the senses.
*Photograph by Klaus Spitzer.*

Fig. 4.47.
In the Open Playground,
wild ornamental and food plants
are common.
*Photograph by Klaus Spitzer.*

Fig. 4.48. The original Environmental Yard 1.5-acre site before transformation. *Photograph by Robin Moore.*

Fig. 4.49.　The Environmental Yard after transformation by the community into a non-formal education site. *Photograph by Robin Moore.*

Fig. 4.50. Elementary grade students playing and learning at the "river" water feature on the Environmental Yard. *Photograph by Robin Moore.*

Fig. 4.51.   A group of children quietly talking in the bushes of the Environmental Yard.
*Photograph by Robin Moore.*

Fig. 4.52.   Children, parents, and teachers working together to transform the playing and learning environment of their school. *Photograph by Robin Moore.*

## New Playgrounds and the Playful City

In many other high-income countries, the concept of the playground has broadened far beyond the traditional stereotype of static manufactured equipment with the sun beating down on it. This image represents but one type of play setting, one that is the most difficult to make accessible to children with disabilities, one that must be scaled to children of different ages, one that must be subjected to stringent safety standards, and one that has little flexibility as a learning resource.

New playgrounds (not so new in some countries) can provide a multidisciplinary base for child development and the creative evolution of local culture. The concept of the Playful City takes this notion one step further to look at all the possible locations and opportunities throughout the urban environment for creating playful, family friendly places with a focus on child development through play.[5]

Two recently documented examples[6] are both in North Carolina. Playport (fig. 4.53) opened in 1992 at Raleigh-Durham Airport. It offers children and accompanying adults a space designed around the theme of taking an airplane trip. By using the cockpit controls, looking out of the airliner window at a scale model from ten thousand feet, up in the control tower, speaking on the intercom, going through security, and sliding over a wing section and engine cowling preflight anxieties can be relieved through dramatic play and a sense of adventure.

Playspace (fig. 4.54) opened in 1991. It is located in the heart of downtown Raleigh in the historic City Market area. The nonprofit facility was started by a group of mothers who wanted an indoor facility where parents could go with their young children to *play* and meet families from all parts of the city in a secure, playful environment. The focus is on dramatic and sensorimotor play from infancy to seven years. Play settings include an infant-toddler corner, a "mainstreet" with play bank, grocery store, emergency room, and lookout; a dress-up/stage area; a manipulative play corner; and sandplay and waterplay settings. Most times during the day, the space is filled to capacity.

Fig. 4.53.   Playport, located in Terminal A, Raleigh-Durham International Airport, provides children and parents with opportunities for dramatic play and relaxation to defuse pre-flight anxiety. *Photograph by Robin Moore.*

Fig. 4.54. Playspace, located in downtown Raleigh, North Carolina, serves children seven years and under and their families. Children and parents or other relatives or caregivers must accompany each other. The focus is on providing dramatic play opportunities related to the everyday environment. There is a Main Street with bank, grocery store and emergency room; a manipulative play area; a dress-up area and stage; an infant-toddler corner; and sand play and water play (the most popular). *Photograph by Robin Moore.*

The central focus of these and other examples of new playgrounds, both indoors and outdoors, is nonformal education, that is, a genuine commitment to and respect for the special culture of childhood that is created through play with adults acting as facilitators, prompters, partners, and providers of tools and materials. Together, children and adults build their own universe in a domain where the formal rules of home and school are suspended, where new imaginary worlds can be created. The experience should be so enjoyable that it far out-competes TV and so stimulating that adult volunteers cannot resist devoting their time and energy to it.

# 5

# PLAYGROUNDS AND EXCEPTIONAL CHILDREN

P lay is as valuable in the cognitive, social, and motor development of children with disabilities as it is for their able-bodied peers. The play of exceptional children is similar in most ways to that of children without disabilities. It serves the same developmental functions and has the same potential for enjoyment and expression.

Play enhances not only physical development but also the cognitive and affective domains. Children with physical disabilities need play to enhance as much as possible the many abilities they possess as well as to facilitate their cognitive and affective development. Play provides an opportunity to interact with the environment, which, according to Piaget, is critical to the development of intelligence. Children need the mental activity involved in play as well as the social interaction.

Play is a vehicle for social mainstreaming children with and without disabilities. Children play for the sake of play: they observe and they interact. Children at play highlight their commonalities. A properly designed playground is conducive to the sharing of experiences and provides a natural avenue for understanding oneself and others. Playgrounds and play settings have the potential to bring together disabled and nondisabled children in shared activities and experiences. In doing so, they can function as powerful tools to mainstream special education populations.

Fig. 5.1. Making the playground accessible to a child with multiple disabilities. The photographs of children in this chapter do not necessarily refer to the different disabilities discussed in each section of this chapter. *Photograph by Michael Carlebach.*

# Playgrounds for All Children

Playgrounds should provide fun and challenge for all children regardless of whether or not they have a disability. In this sense, playgrounds are universal and democratic structures. Their design must include forms that provide and integrate the play experience of all children. A well-designed playground should provide opportunities for exercise, discovery, and challenge for all children, no matter what their limitations are. This approach is known as universal design.[1]

A 1979 survey revealed that there were very few playgrounds specifically designed for individuals with disabilities. Most play facilities that were available for special needs populations were segregated according to specific types of disabilities.[2]

Programmed into any playground and its equipment should be different levels of challenge and individual options. For all children, playground activities should provide a high degree of flexibility rather than be specific for certain disabilities.

Playgrounds designed to accommodate children with and without disabilities present two major challenges.

1. Equipment must be developed or modified to be accessible to all children.
2. Other types of play settings where children can experience and benefit from contact with each other must be available.[3]

The following examples of playgrounds have been designed for all children:

1. The Demas Playground, New City, New York, is being used by children with and without disabilities primarily as a place where they can develop the ability to play. It includes sand and water tables, a modified slide, a climbing frame, and a series of playlofts. Wheelchairs can be locked onto a merry-go-round that can be turned by hand. Ramps enable children using crutches or wheelchairs to explore areas independently.[4]

Fig. 5.2.   Making playgrounds in park-like settings accessible to children using wheel-chairs. *Photograph by Michael Carlebach.*

2. The Jamaica Plain, Massachusetts, playground at the Language and Cognitive Development Center is for children ages two to eight who are autistic, emotionally disordered, or brain injured and have severe communication and interaction difficulties. This playground is also used by neighborinig children. The playground equipment provides problems for children to solve.[5]

3. The creative play area at Cleveland Heights, Ohio, brings able-bodied children and children with disabilities, along with their parents, together to play and interact. Towers at all four corners of the play area are linked together by long wooden ramps. Slides have ramps next to them so children using wheelchairs can crawl up the ramp and then go down the slide.[6]

4. Mesa, Arizona, has a neighborhood park that provides opportunities for disabled and able-bodied individuals to enjoy leisure time activities together at the same facility. The park is totally accessible to all individuals, including barrier-free exercise trails and graded levels of difficulty.[7]

5. A local community group representing the recreational needs of people with disabilities initiated the redesign of a large children's playground as part of the renovation of Flood Park, a WPA project in Menlo Park, California (figs. 4.10, 4.11, 4.12). The playground design was based on the play settings described in *The Play For All Guidelines*.[8] It incorporated many ideas from local users and residents, including children, solicited through a series of community planning workshops.[9] The playground contains many innovative features accessible to children and adults of all abilities. These include an entry area with orienting elements such as a tactile map and a landmark tower with wind chimes, a very popular water play feature, a multilevel accessible sand play terrace, and a fantasy play area; also included are a manufactured play equipment area, a performance stage, a multipurpose meadow, and a special multisetting zone for infant play. A series of visual, auditory, olfactory, and tactile cues helps orient users with sensory impairments as they move around the site.

Fig. 5.3.
Children with
and without disabilities
meeting on the playground.
*Photograph by Michael Carlebach.*

When planning a playground for students with disabilities, it is important to be aware of the types of handicapping conditions affecting the population who will use the facility. Cook, Tessier, and Armbruster define the following nine categories of exceptional students:

1. Deaf and hearing impaired.
2. Mentally retarded.
3. Orthopedically impaired.
4. Seriously emotionally disturbed.
5. Specific learning disability.
6. Speech impaired.
7. Visually impaired.
8. Other health impaired.
9. Multiplihandicapped.[10]

Doctors, physical therapists, recreation therapists, and parents of handicapped children can help design playgrounds for children with disabilities. Concerns include the amount of supervision needed, safety requirements, physical limitations of each disability, what children enjoy doing, what activities would help them develop, and what activities should be avoided.

General design considerations include the following:

1. Interesting enough to attract all children.
2. Range of activities from passive games to active sports.
3. Multiple levels of excitement from activities that calm to those that stimulate.
4. Multiple levels of skills to encourage children to try new challenges.
5. Durability.
6. Use of prototypical equipment that can be easily modified, for example, swings with an extra supporting strap across the back, slides with extra high sides, or handholds on climbing equipment.[11]

Six levels of a recreational curriculum for developmentally disabled persons were described by Wehman. They included toy play (blocks, dolls, sandbox, puppets), passive leisure (books, radios, puzzles), game activities (forts, ramps, hiding places), sports (mats, climbing areas, tennis and bas-

Fig. 5.4.
A specially adapted swing
for children using wheelchairs.
*Photograph by Michael Carlebach.*

ketball courts), hobby activities (models, art materials, gardens), and socialization (provided by group activities).[12]

Children with special needs are often less adept at developing the skills other children acquire naturally through play. They need more structured activities and appropriate toys and play materials. Toys need to be durable enough to withstand harsh treatment and must be appropriate to the developmental level of the child. Because children with special needs are often at a developmental level considerably below their chronological ages, toys and play materials must be appropriately chosen.[13]

Often, play structures frustrate children with disabilities. A mainstreaming structure is one that is designed for both disabled and nondisabled children to provide both physical and mental challenges for all stages of development and accessibility to all children. These play structures are designed to accommodate disabled children with activities and challenges that are as normal as possible.

Any structure, whether mainstream or exclusively for the disabled, needs space for activity, interaction, rest, and adult supervision. Several entrances and exits should be provided so that slower children are not in the way of faster or more able children. Such structures also need spacious decks where children can rest yet still be involved with play activities or where children with severe motor disabilities can be vicariously involved in the play activities. The structure needs to be accessible to adults, so they can easily assist children. Benches for observation need to be close enough to be effective but not intrusive.

Safety is a big issue with disabled children, but overprotection limits their play and their involvement with the environment. Children will generally stay within their comfort levels and do what is within their physical limits.

A structure can be fairly low to the ground and still be interesting if it is complex enough to provide a variety of activities.

Handholds should be strategically placed for children who may need to stabilize themselves.

Safety surfaces must be installed around and under the play structures. Pathways for wheelchairs and crutches must be hard enough to support

Fig. 5.5.   Playground equipment that can be used by a wide range of children. *Photograph by Michael Carlebach.*

them. Play structures should allow for as much independent play as possible. Walking and crawling areas should be covered with resilient paving like that used in running tracks.[14]

Jambor and Gargiulo observe that most playgrounds are still not meeting the needs of the approximately 12 percent of the school-age population who exhibit special needs. They suggest that to develop appropriate playgrounds planners consider the following:

1. Children are more likely to have accidents if space is limited.
2. Handrails should be provided, especially on slopes.
3. Maneuvering on uneven surfaces or loose surfaces, such as gravel or bark, can be a problem.
4. Private intimate spaces are important, especially for children with disabilities.
5. Seating with backs and armrests should be provided throughout the area for children with special needs and their parents.
6. Easy access to shelter from sun and rain should be provided.[15]

A barrier-free environment can increase the independence of disabled persons (both children and parents with disabilities). Mobility barriers are conditions in the environment that restrict or prevent free interchange or movement by individuals attempting to use facilities. Often only slight modifications will make otherwise inaccessible facilities accessible for the disabled. It is important to identify areas that restrict use of facilities and to modify them.[16]

Playgrounds must provide an adequate range of experience and some measure of control. Materials should be under the control of the children. Disabled children should be able to throw, carry, sift, spill, splash, and pile materials just as all children do. Water and sand are the best materials for them to use in this type of play.

Another way to exercise control is to rearrange the environment. Paper, glue, paint, rope, tires, spools, blocks, cartons, and so forth, all lend themselves to rearrangement.

Moving things in the environment provides yet another way to make it possible for disabled children to exercise control. Swings and other traditional equipment provide predictable movement, but other activities such as ropes and suspended nets may be more easily manipulated by children with special needs and, therefore, be more appropriate for them. The ability to move over, under, around, and through something also gives all children a sense of control.

Control also means changing one's mind about involvement in a risky activity. Slides, for example, should have a way to get off without backing down the ladder. Thus, a slide on a platform may have a ramp that provides an alternate way off an apparatus.

Choice also gives a sense of control to children. They need not only to be able to choose what type of activity to participate in but also whether to play alone, in small groups, or with a large group. Therefore, different types of spaces must be provided.[17]

A playground that provides no new challenges will not provide new learning. Too great a challenge, however, can be overwhelming. Therefore, the playground should provide a series of graded challenges. This arrangement not only gives children a continuum of challenges to work toward but also allows children of different levels of development to play next to each other.

When designing appropriate play settings usable by all children, planners should remember that the more general the form of an object, the more choice children have in how they will use it. Children must be free to make mistakes and to fall without being overprotected — this is true for all children. Physical, mental, and emotional problems often overlap, but there are usually some abilities that can be encouraged. In the following sections we look at various needs more specifically.

### Mentally Retarded Children and Playground Needs

Mentally retarded children need an environment that they can shape and influence for themselves. They need a series of activities of varying complexity so they can see the effect they have on their environment.

Equipment and activities for mildly mentally retarded children need very little modification from normally developing children in equipment and activities. Severely retarded individuals need an array of activities that are developmentally appropriate. Full enclosure of the playground is especially important for severely retarded children so they do not wander away.

Research on the behavioral effects of architecture and environment has indicated that some behaviors are characteristic of an environment rather than of an individual. A play environment should discourage undesirable behaviors, such as self-abuse, self-stimulation, and aggression of severely and profoundly retarded persons. Such a playground needs to balance safety needs, materials, preference for certain activities, and other special requirements.[18]

Special problems in conjunction with playgrounds for severely and profoundly retarded populations are addressed by the following:

1. Covering structures with materials that can be mopped and withstand use of strong cleaning agents.
2. Creating areas that are easy to reach by several routes and can be seen from the outside.
3. Covering the edges of walls and ramps with metal strips so they are difficult to take apart.[19]

The educational needs of the severely and profoundly retarded are addressed by the following:

1. Creating structures that are brightly colored to attract children to different activities.
2. Using color-coded systems to help them differentiate various types of activities.
3. Using ramps to draw children up into play structures. Interlocking pathways so that once children enter a structure they can continue into other areas.
4. Using switches that activate either visual or auditory stimuli strategically placed so they can be used to establish cause and effect relations.

Fig. 5.6.   Playing together. *Photograph by Michael Carlebach.*

5. Providing tactile stimulation through the use of obstacle courses created by using materials with various textures.
6. Providing a wide range of motor activity through the use of gradually sloping ramps for crawling, rolling, sitting, and crouching. Ramps of this type should be enclosed by high walls to avoid child falls.[20]

Playgrounds for trainable retarded children should:
1. Strengthen physical and intellectual abilities.
2. Enhance the development of receptive and expressive language.
3. Facilitate verbal communication to express needs and feelings.
4. Promote independence by providing an environment that they can manipulate.
5. Enrich motor, academic, and social development.
6. Foster recreational and creative play.[21]

Playground designs for trainable retarded children should use the following:
1. Structures to allow children to negotiate equipment in their own ways. For example, making provisions so that steps can be crawled under as well as walked up.
2. Traditional equipment, such as swings, ropes, and seesaws, which enable children to transfer skills to other settings.
3. Multimedia approaches to provide experiences in tactile and sensory stimulation as well as academic and motor experiences.[22]

## Emotionally Disturbed

Emotionally disturbed children may be unable to judge their limitations and may be overly cautious or try to go beyond their abilities. Their perception may be distorted, and they may manifest self-destructive behavior. Emotionally disturbed children need facilities where they can learn about themselves and the world safely. Their environment should be reassuring and unambiguous. Areas should be manageable in size and well-defined. Emotionally disturbed

Fig. 5.7.
Dunk shot.
*Photograph by Michael Carlebach.*

children need playground settings that allow them to break away easily from threatening activities. They should be provided with opportunities to observe activities without participating unless they want to.[23]

## Hearing Impaired

Children with hearing impairments need a play environment that concentrates on the other senses. Playground areas for deaf children must have potential hazards fully in view and have guard rails around movement apparatus. Playgrounds should include design elements that make it possible for adults supervising deaf children to visually communicate with them.[24]

## Visually Impaired

Play structures for children with visual impairments should have entrances, exits, and edges marked in a way that can be felt and identified. Railings in critical areas are also important.

The visually impaired need a sensory-rich environment with physical cues that encourage them to develop balance and direction and heighten their senses of touch and hearing. Auditory clues, such as chimes, help to orient the visually impaired. Tactile maps and braille descriptions of each area can be helpful, while the use of bright colors and sharp contrasts for partially sighted children can be valuable. Visually impaired children need to be carefully supervised around moving equipment and when climbing on equipment.[25]

## Orthopedically Impaired

Children with orthopedic impairments need playground settings and activities that (1) arrest the deterioration of their existing abilities, (2) strengthen skills that can be developed, and (3) provide them with alternate or compensatory skills.[26]

Features for playgrounds that are particularly important for orthopedically impaired children include

1. Climbing frames similar to a jungle gym with grasp bars next to a playloft.
2. Drinking fountains accessible to children using wheelchairs.
3. Playlofts interconnected with stairs and ramps with hiding spaces underneath that are large enough for children using wheelchairs.
4. Ramps with handrails connecting all levels of playloft areas with the ground. (Ramp gradients should be no greater than 1:12; 1:15 is better.)
5. A sandbox with a variety of edge conditions at ground and wheelchair levels.
6. Water tables of various heights with indentations for wheelchairs.
7. Wheelchair paths that include traffic signs and signals.
8. Tunnels for crawling, large enough to accommodate wheelchairs.
9. Nonskid sidewalks or walkways with surfaces hard enough and wide enough to accommodate passage of wheelchairs, crutches, or braces.[27]

## Conclusion

The needs of children with disabilities in playground settings can best be met by clearly understanding their strengths and limitations. Playgrounds should provide the maximum opportunity and challenge under the safest possible conditions. An ideal playground for exceptional children should aim to provide the same play experiences as a well-designed playground for children without disabilities. The ideal solution is a universally designed play space for all children containing a broad range of play settings other than traditional play equipment. Up-to-date sources of guidance exist for the design of this type of play area.[28]

# 6

# PLAYGROUND CONSTRUCTION

# AND SAFETY

S afety is one of the most important issues in the design and use of playgrounds. Although risk taking is an important part of most playground activities, it does not have to be associated with hazardous and dangerous conditions. The dangers caused by poorly installed equipment, bad equipment design, poor maintenance, and the use of hard surfaces underneath and around playground equipment can all be avoided. In this chapter, we provide an overview on playground safety and suggestions for improving playground safety, design, and use.

### What Are the Most Common Accidents in Playground Settings?

In a detailed study of accidents treated at the Toronto Hospital for Sick Children for the period June 15 – September 30, 1975, of the 122 cases involving playground equipment, in 21, or 17.2 percent, equipment was the probable cause.[1]

According to the Consumer Product Safety Commission, approximately 170,000 injuries requiring emergency room treatment occurred on playgrounds in 1988 (the most recent year for which data have been published). About three-fourths of these accidents on both public and home playground equipment resulted from falls. For public playground equipment, 58 percent of injuries involved falls to the surface below the equipment. Other types of falls accounted for just over 16 percent. Of all public playground injuries, 29 percent of injuries were lacerations, 28 percent were fractures, and 22 percent contusions and abrasions. Injuries most frequently occurred on climbers (32%), slides (29%), and swings (26%).[2]

An almost totally safe play environment can be created by going to extraordinary lengths to avoid any type of risk. The problem with such a setting is that it lacks most of the important elements necessary for meaningful play. These include variety, complexity, challenge, risk, flexibility, and adaptability.[3]

Some risk is, therefore, inevitable in almost any playground setting. But risk factors can be minimized with the implementation of a well-thought-out safety program. Wilkinson and Lockhart maintain that any safety program has two major goals. "The first is to eliminate serious types of injuries, e.g., strangulations, skull fractures, concussions and causes of death or dismemberment. The second is to minimize other minor types of injuries, e.g., broken bones, abrasions, lacerations, or punctures."[4] Meeting these goals can be accomplished by eliminating hard surfaces and potential entrapment features, constructing equipment from safe and durable materials, maintaining equipment, educating children about the proper use of equipment, and establishing performance standards that all playground equipment is required to meet.[5]

## How Safe Are Playgrounds?

Several well-publicized cases of death and serious injury in playground accidents, massive awards to the plaintiffs, and an independently developing liability crisis have brought the issue of playground safety to the forefront. City officials, staff, designers, manufacturers — all those involved in the provision and staffing of children's playgrounds — are apprehensive. But part of the apprehension has been bred from a lack of information describing both the general and detailed picture of playground safety.

A more accurate picture is needed of playground injuries compared with injuries in the child environment as a whole. In 1984, 4,300 accidental deaths occurred to five-to-fourteen-year-olds in the United States (a rate of

12.7/100,000 population). Of these, 2,300 (6.8/100,000) were motor-vehicle related (and, of these, 1,070 or 3.2/100,000 involved pedestrians); 1,100 (3.2/100,000) occurred in the public environment but were not vehicle related; 800 (2.4/100,000) were home related; and 100 (0.3/100,000) were work related.[6] Between 1973 and 1989 it was estimated that 276 children were killed on American playgrounds or about seventeen deaths per year.[7] This means that the chance of being killed at home or in the street as a pedestrian are roughly forty-seven to sixty-three times greater than the chance of being killed on a playground. Motor vehicles as a whole are about 135 times more lethal than playgrounds.

By narrowing the scope of the safety issue to school environments, where children spend the most amount of time, what is the comparative safety record of play settings? In 1985, the National Safety Council reported on 15,000 K−12 accidents for 8,600 school jurisdictions for the 1983−1984 school year. They quoted rates per 100,000 K−6 student days as follows: equipment-related accidents, 0.42; ball playing, 0.18; running, 0.31; and miscellaneous accidents (including those on wall, fences, steps, and walks), 0.54. The rate for all school-related accidents for grades K−6 was 4.92. The rate for all building-related accidents was 1.40 while for physical-education-related accidents was 1.04. In other words, equipment-related accidents accounted for about one-tenth of all accidents in the school environment and were less than one-third as frequent as accidents inside the school building (i.e., on stairs, with lockers, in classrooms, auditoriums, washrooms, and toilets). These data tell us that several school settings are a source of serious injury, including schoolyard play equipment.[8]

Boyce, Subolewski, Sprunger, and Schaeffer in a 1984 study of playground equipment injuries in the Tucson Unified School District reported a total of 2,193 injuries over a two-year period in a school district population of 28,636 elementary school students. Of these, 511 injuries (23.3 percent) involved the use of playground equipment. One-quarter of these injuries were severe, including concussions, crush wounds, fractures, and multiple injuries. Boyce and his colleagues found that their research confirmed earlier studies that climbing-related injuries tended to be more severe than other types of injuries.[9]

149

Fig. 6.1.
Using a slide in an unintended way.
*Photograph by Michael Carlebach.*

150

## Minimizing Accidents on Playgrounds

The great majority of accidents that occur on playgrounds are avoidable. They occur because of poor maintenance or lack of supervision or because children misuse equipment. This happens most frequently when children are not instructed on the proper use of playground apparatus or when they are left unsupervised.

Good maintenance of play areas is essential. This relies on a program of regular, standardized safety inspections as a routine risk-management procedure.

As mentioned, some degree of risk is inevitable in any playground setting. An important part of playground play involves risk taking, testing one's limits, and trying physical activities one has never undertaken before. Thus, pulling oneself up on a jungle gym in a traditional playground, or putting a roof on a hand-built shack are perfectly normal activities that include some degree of risk. Minor cuts and bruises are going to be part of any normal play situation. What is important is to minimize the risk of more serious injuries.

With a slide, for example, protective rails must be provided up the ladder and along its sides to prevent children from falling off. The landing area at the bottom of the slide should be cushioned with loose sand, wood chips, or other shock-absorbing surfacing material.[10] If erosion is creating depressions in the playground surface, these should be filled and covered with a soft, loose surface material. Children using the slide should be instructed in its proper use. Pushing, shoving, taking turns out of order all create the potential for accidents. Connecting parts, concrete footings, and so forth, should be periodically checked to make sure that there are no loose parts or sharp, protruding edges. Handholds and rungs should have their bolts tightened.

Safety problems differ with the type of playground. In traditional playgrounds, for example, most injuries occur because equipment is misused or because of poor maintenance. Otherwise safe equipment becomes dangerous when used improperly. For example, a child climbing up the support legs of a slide not only runs the risk of falling onto a hard and uncushioned surface but also of being stepped on by someone else using the apparatus. Going down a

Fig. 6.2.　A climbing apparatus being safely used. *Photograph by Michael Carlebach.*

slide head first is another example of how equipment can be misused. Soft surfaces placed at the bottom of a slide that can safely cushion a child coming down feet first obviously will not work for a child coming down head first. Poor maintenance can lead to exposed sharp edges on metal support pieces, the loss of rounded caps on potentially dangerous extrusions, and loose anchored support pieces and ladders.

Designer, adventure, and creative playgrounds tend to be less accident prone than traditional playgrounds but have unique problems as well. With these playgrounds, children are more likely to be using special tools and materials and found objects. Careful instruction and supervision in the use of tools and materials is necessary. Potentially dangerous materials must be properly processed and used. A two-by-four with nails sticking out from it, for example, is a potentially useful object for recycling in an adventure playground setting. Making sure that it is carefully recycled, stored, and used is obviously important.

Problems with equipment and design are not the only cause of accidents on playgrounds. Human error is also an important factor. Children must be taught that equipment should be used responsibly in accordance with the original intentions of its designers. This is not to suggest that children cannot determine new uses of equipment and materials for themselves but that they must do so in a responsible and critically aware context. For example, if a group of children want to take a hanging and climbing apparatus such as a jungle gym and drape sheets or blankets over it to make a tent, then they cannot do so while other children are using the device for climbing and hanging activities.

Children need to be made aware that overcrowding on the slide or having too many people "hanging" around a climbing area—possibly participating in other activities—can lead to potential accidents. Overcrowding tends to lead to more accidents in playground settings, for example, a child runs away from another child as part of a game or "fooling around" straight into a moving swing or other device.

Safety is often ignored in many playground settings in exchange for aesthetic and maintenance considerations. Using hard asphalt may take less

Fig. 6.3.
The see-saw, a traditional
and often unsafe play apparatus.
*Photograph by Michael Carlebach.*

upkeep and look neater than loose wood chips, but it provides a lethal surface under climbing apparatus. Soft mats for children to land on are subject to wear and tear and, if left unsupervised, are at greater risk of being vandalized and misused.

When purchasing playground equipment the following guidelines should be taken into account:

1. Make sure that the equipment has no sharp edges that can cause cuts or tears. All openings should be closed and all corners should have rounded or smoothed edges. Sloppy milling or finishing work may leave rough exposed areas. If the surface feels extremely rough, the equipment probably will cause problems.

2. Make sure that there are no dangerous extrusions. In wooden playgrounds, particularly, this is a potential problem. Besides the risk of running into extrusions at eye level, children may accidentally hook the strings of their coat hoods on a protrusion and strangle themselves.

3. Make sure that equipment is structured so that children cannot become entrapped. Avoid equipment with small holes that children can catch hands or fingers in, rungs and bars that they can get caught in if they are pushed or fall through in some unnatural way.

4. Make sure swings are suspended by proper bearings, not simple "S" hooks that can be pulled open and become a serious hazard.

5. Be sure that all climbing equipment has guardrails and protective barriers.

6. Check all moving parts to be certain that children cannot get their hands or feet or clothing caught.[11]

### Safety Surfacing: A Special Problem in Playground Design

Developing safe surface areas on which children can play represents one of the most difficult issues faced by playground designers and builders. Accident data indicates that 60 percent of all injuries occur when individuals come in violent contact with playground surfaces. In most instances this occurs as a result of falls from equipment.[12] Accidents involving contact with paved surfaces occur much more frequently than surfaces made of resilient material.

Surfaces such as sand, gravel, and wood chips are superior to paved surface areas but are frequently avoided in playground design because they are more difficult to care for and, in many instances, are not as aesthetically pleasing as other types of surfaces. The question that must primarily concern those responsible for playground settings is not one of aesthetics but of safety. In this context, resilient playground surfaces are essential to improving playground safety.

## Conclusion

Many factors affect the development of greater playground safety. Good design is obviously an essential factor, as is proper maintenance and the training of supervisory staff and the children in appropriate use of a particular setting's equipment and resources. Minor injuries are inevitable in most playground settings, just as such injuries are part of the experience of day-to-day life. More severe accidents should be rare indeed if necessary precatuions and procedures are followed.

# 7

# EDUCATIONAL AND RECREATIONAL

# USES OF PLAYGROUNDS

## AN ACTIVITY APPROACH

In this chapter we outline the ways in which playgrounds can be used as part of nonformal and formal education. Playground settings have the potential for a wide range of activities and learning experiences for children — experiences that can challenge them not only physically but in fundamental ways in their cognitive and affective development.

No single right way exists to set up an educational program on a playground. Variables of space, equipment, and the developmental level of the children will contribute to making each situation unique. In this chapter we suggest ways to help teachers make maximum use of different playground settings for both learning and fun. Obviously, many of the suggestions included here can be adapted by playground supervisors and parents to meet their particular needs.

Teachers have an important role in the success or failure of any playground program. Their principal task is to prepare the environment for play, observe what happens in that environment, and then decide what action needs to be taken either to modify the environment or interact with the children.

### Preparing the Environment

As noted previously in the research of Frost and Campbell, children prefer complex play structures that offer several play options as well as equipment that is movable and does something. Children also prefer play equipment that can be changed to meet the requirements of their play, rather than having to adjust their play to conform to the structures. Provision of this type of equipment is a major step in promoting the play process.

Creative play is encouraged by providing unstructured equipment and allowing children to use this equipment in creative and unconventional ways. The play area should be appealing, and materials should be accessible.

In addition to concerns about equipment, it is important to consider the use of natural settings and materials whenever possible. Living environments that contain vegetation, water, soil, and wildlife offer tremendous opportunities for learning. Even a playground with apparently few animals or plant life can be teeming with materials such as small insects, transient birds, and wild plants, which can be used as the basis for a wide range of learning experiences for children.

When organizing play, it is essential that teachers not only clearly understand the potential and limitations of the environment but also the cognitive and motor development of the children with whom they are working. They must take differences into account, depending on whether the play setting is intended for toddlers, preschoolers, elementary, or middle school students.

### Toddlers

In contrast to older children, toddlers are still enjoying sensory play, but they are also interested in testing and using their developing motor skills. Imitating behavior gives way to pretend play. Children at this age like activities that provide them with opportunities for exploration and experimentation. Toddlers need simple play materials that can be used in many different ways rather than toys that dictate what can be done or that simply make children spectators. Imaginary and pretend experiences are important for children in this age group.

### Preschoolers

Preschoolers need active engagement with the physical environment. From this interaction with the environment and with other people, they need to learn to feel effective and competent. They need to be able to handle their environments independently and discover for themselves that there is more than one way to accomplish something. They need to be able to balance their need for challenge against their need for safety. They can also learn the self-control necessary to regulate their own behavior. Cognitively, children of this age are learning symbolic expression. Therefore, they need lots of symbolic and pretend play. Logical thought, particularly conservation and classification, is also developing, so activities that help them discover relationships are important. They need activities that foster creativity and problem solving and promote increased attention span and task involvement. Children between the ages of three and five still need large motor activities as well as those that develop fine motor skills.

*Elementary School*

Elementary school-age children are usually eager to participate in activities and group games that include physical activity. By the age of six or seven years, children are proficient at throwing and catching balls, hopping, jumping, and climbing. Between eight and ten years of age children have the balance, coordination, and strength to enable them to participate in gymnastics and team sports. Some children develop motor skills earlier than others, and some are more genetically predisposed toward developing better coordination or more strength than others. Motivation and practice are very important in children's acquisition of motor skills.

Socially, peers become increasingly more important as children move from preschool through the school years. Older children like to spend more time with peers, and peer influence becomes more important as children go into middle and senior high school. Therefore, playgrounds for elementary school-age children should provide equipment for practicing balance, coordination, and strength as well as areas for group games and social interaction with peers.

*Middle School*

There is a major transition between elementary and middle school yet school designs and, more specifically, playground designs frequently do not support middle school students sufficiently. Middle school environments are often the same as those provided for high school students even though middle school students are developmentally quite different. Outdoor areas for this age group should include the following: ample space for movement; areas for exploration; a wide variety of easily accessible materials; activity areas for hobbies and interest groups; large spaces for vigorous body movement; environmental flexibility and space for socialization. Adventure playgrounds are particularly appropriate for this age group because they allow children to explore freely, experience the consequences and results of their actions, and learn at speeds and levels with which they feel comfortable.

*Students with Special Needs*

Teachers working with children who have special needs should be sensitive to the extent to which activities may need to be modified. The developmental age of these children is a more accurate guide to the level of play activities than their chronological age. Diverse playground settings provide teachers with unusual opportunities to extend the physical world and experience of children with special needs, but sometimes teachers need to devise extraordinary ways to encourage the play of these children. A playground can introduce a physically or mentally challenged child to a whole new world of activity, social interaction, problem solving, and autonomous decision making.

*Playground Safety*

Making sure that a playground is a safe place for children to play is a basic responsibility of the teacher. In this context, using common sense is the best guide. It is obviously important to check the play area carefully before the children arrive. Materials failure as well as vandalized equipment result in safety

Fig. 7.1.
Testing one's physical limits.
*Photograph by Michael Carlebach.*

161

Fig. 7.2.
Hanging around on the jungle gym.
*Photograph by Michael Carlebach.*

162

problems. Important also, particularly with younger children, is the need to see if miscellaneous pieces of equipment have been dropped or left in places that pose hazards. For example, a toy metal truck left at the base of a slide could injure a child who slides down and lands on it.

## The Teacher as Observer

Because hazards can often occur as children are playing, it is important that teachers be constantly alert for potential problems. Teachers should also be sensitive to children misusing equipment. A slide when properly used is safe and can provide exciting experiences for children. When a child, however, jumps off the ladder, or otherwise misuses the equipment, the risk for injury is greatly increased. Without restricting or inhibiting play, teachers working in playground settings need to be constantly on guard against equipment being used dangerously. Although it is important to welcome unconventional use of equipment and to encourage imaginative substitutions whenever possible, these alternative uses should not pose a danger for children. Teachers need to find an intelligent balance between constructive risk taking and concerns for safety.

From observation, teachers can learn whether more time, space, or play materials are needed, whether certain materials are beyond a child's ability, or if the play situation is not sufficiently stimulating. In addition to having abundant play materials, children need extended periods to engage in self-chosen and self-directed activities. Teachers should intervene in a play situation only after they have determined through careful observation that intervention will enhance children's play experiences.

Playgrounds provide an excellent opportunity to informally observe children's activities. Information and insights about children and their needs can be garnered by observing patterns of behavior and activity on the playground. Systematically observing the social interaction of children when they play, seeing what problems they have in handling certain physical activities, and examining difficulties in problem solving can all increase teachers' understanding. Types of behavior that cannot be observed in the classroom can be seen in the playground setting. It is difficult, for example, in most classrooms to evaluate how a child spontaneously interacts with other children. On the playground, with its natural and free environment, the child as explorer and social being becomes more visible. In such settings, teachers can develop a clearer sense of the abilities and limitations of individual children.

### Teacher Intervention

The playground provides an ideal situation for cooperative learning both across developmental levels and across other differences. Cooperative play activities sensitize children to one another's needs and to their similarities with one another. Playground activities can also provide teachers with opportunities to promote gender fairness and equity. Playleaders can introduce boys who always organize and control play, to the idea of sharing and cooperating and negate the distinction between "boys' activities" and "girls' activities."

Teachers should be aware that unstructured free play can lead to hostile and aggressive behavior on the part of certain children, particularly those who lack self-control. It may be helpful to structure play opportunities for impulsive children in such a way that they have choices but do not end up in situations where they can lose control. The teacher as playground observer needs to monitor and redirect play before it escalates into hostile behavior.

### Playgrounds and the Cognitive Domain

Playground settings that encourage exploration and discovery can promote important experiences in the cognitive domain. Problem-solving skills — a high priority, particularly in the math and science curriculum at all levels of the educational system — can be exercised in many different ways in playground settings. A teacher can encourage exploration and problem solving by providing settings that can be used in many different ways by children.

The teacher can promote problem-solving behavior in students by carefully timing questions and offers of help. The right question at the right time can significantly extend the child's investigation. Through successfully solving problems in playground settings children are able to develop positive self-concepts and a sense of empowerment.

The boring and mundane aspects of playground maintenance can provide constructive learning experiences for children. Hauling toys and various play equipment to the playground and, when play ends, putting these materials away can provide important classification experiences. For example, children can learn to put away sand toys by storing shovels, pails, and sifters on shelves according to use or size. Such tasks represent important first steps in categorizing and classifying. Similarly, children share responsibility as part of these activities, an important benefit from the management and distribution of materials.

### The Classroom Connection: Suggested Playground Activities

The possibilities offered by playground environments for discovery and learning are enormous. The list that follows is intended to suggest some of the many ways that playgrounds can provide positive experiences for children. The list is by no means comprehensive, but instead intended to help the reader begin to think about the many ways that playgrounds can be used to enhance children's learning.

    1. Set up sand and water play areas as part of an outdoor playground. Construct large sandboxes or sand play areas with wide ledges around the outside to serve as seats or tables for activities. Place the sandbox far away from the door so less sand is tracked indoors and keep it covered when it is not in use. Sand is good for pouring, molding, and construction. Pails, shovels, trucks, funnels, containers, and other props help children in their imaginative activities. Water play can take place with a water table, a washtub, or other large container. Children should wear plastic aprons and

Fig. 7.3.
Making it to the top.
*Photograph by Michael Carlebach.*

boots or plastic bags over their shoes. Supervise sand and water play to keep children from throwing sand and splashing water on each other, but do not restrict them unreasonably in these areas. They should be free to enjoy these activities.

2. Encourage children to use sand play areas to build scale models or maps of the neighborhoods in which they live. Have them describe the different areas after they have built them or explain how to get from one place to another.

3. Use the imaginary landscapes that children spontaneously create in sand play areas as a vehicle of communication between children and teacher. Children can use a sand play area to design an imaginary city or town, which can be from any period in history or culture or from the past, present, or future. Explore with them the different components of their town or city (walls, roads, rivers, etc.).

4. Help children plant gardens and tend to them over an extended period. Use rates of growth to help children develop numerical and measurement skills. Observations of weather, climactic and seasonal changes, and cycles of growth and decay can be powerful motivators for learning. The status of "garden wildlife" and phenomena such as insect metamorphosis are fascinating to children.

5. Set up a woodworking center in a supervised area of the playground where children can practice using tools such as hammers, screwdrivers, and saws to make simple objects or invent things for themselves. Birdhouses and windmill devices are good examples. Teach the children to use the tools properly and supervise them at all times. The value of woodworking is the experience and the creative process, not the product.

6. Encourage children to participate in pretend play by providing natural settings and props such as sturdy boxes, boards, and ladders.

7. Set up science activities in outdoor play areas using materials such as water, pulleys, ropes, and plants and animals.

Fig. 7.4.
Animals in the playground setting.
*Photograph by Michael Carlebach.*

8. Give children colored chalks to create large murals and drawings on a flat, hard surface. Asphalt provides a good surface for this type of activity, and if chalk is used, it will quickly wash off with the first rain.

9. Encourage children to participate in games such as hopscotch which can be painted on appropriate playground surfaces. Children can learn sequence and order as well as how to follow instructions and rules through playing these types of games.

10. Have children examine the soil on the playground. They can sift it and/or check to see where puddles collect.

11. Ask the children to count all the living things on the playground and then enumerate all the nonliving things. They can invent their own categories, such as humanmade objects, natural forms, color, shape, size, length, hard/soft, or texture.

12. Give children sheets of paper on which are listed categories, such as animals and plants. Ask them to identify a predetermined number of objects or as many as they can find on the playground in each category.

13. Set out a specified number of objects (e.g., a rubber ball, a spoon, an old glove) that can be searched for by a group of children. Organize teams and select a prize for the group that can collect the most objects. Emphasize the use of systematic methods as the children search. Help children invent their own treasure hunts with clues that they develop.

14. Have children ask their parents or older relatives, such as grandparents, what types of games and activities they played on playgrounds when they were children. Help children compile lists of activities and rules for games they can use in their own playground settings.

15. Create an obstacle course using tunnels or tubes for climbing in and out or construct other play areas with different types of levels, in which children must climb in and out, up and over according to a specified order. Discuss their feelings of different spatial relationships.

16. Introduce special materials, such as soap bubbles, as a special activity or event on the playground. Have children compete to see who can blow the largest bubble or use a watch to time how long a bubble lasts or measure how far it can travel before it pops.
17. Have children use materials you have collected to construct simple tents or roofed areas on selected areas of the playground.
18. Have children measure change in a natural form such as a plant. Take measurements over time to determine changes in the height of the plant, and breadth of a leaf, or the length of a branch.
19. Have children catalog all of the animals (insects, birds, small mammals, etc.) found on the playground. Ask them to describe how each is different from or the same as the others (movement, size, color, shape, etc.).
20. Observe birds with the children on the playground. Ask them to imitate bird movements as a class activity. Have them draw pictures of the different birds they see or write descriptions or poems about them.
21. Have children estimate the area covered by their playground or classroom. Ask them to explain how they made their estimates. Then help them carefully measure the areas and see how correct their estimates were.
22. Provide children with hand-held magnifiers. Have them observe tiny objects that they cannot easily see with normal vision. Have them observe how certain objects like seeds and dust tend to clump together. Have them observe how small plants grow differently when in the open as compared to along the edge of a wall, and so forth.
23. Have children go out and listen to the sounds on the playground for fifteen or twenty minutes then list all the sounds they heard. Back in the classroom have children write descriptions of the sounds they listed and then see if other children can identify the sounds from the descriptions.

Fig. 7.5.
Getting into the swing of things.
*Photograph by Michael Carlebach.*

171

24. Measure the trees on the playground and draw pictures of them. Measure the shadows they make at different times of the day. Discuss with children why the length of the shadows changes throughout the day.
25. Find two similar but different objects on the playground, such as two flowers from different plants or two leaves from the same plant. Have children list how the objects are different or the same. Have them write descriptions of the similarities and differences.

# 8

# CONCLUSION

## CALL FOR ACTION

In this work we examine issues related to play theory, the historical development of playgrounds, current research on playgrounds, innovative playgrounds, playgrounds and special education, and the educational and recreational use of playgrounds.

In this final chapter, we explore the potential of playgrounds as a means of improving educational impact on the development of children. In particular, we want to present the possibilities that playgrounds hold for extending the experience of children in inner-city neighborhoods. Almost all of what we are proposing is applicable to other settings and children's needs. We emphasize the inner-city setting, however, because of the greater need of children who live there and the potential that playgrounds in these neighborhoods have to improve the quality of their lives significantly — the lives of some of America's poorest and most neglected children.

Following the lead of the Declaration of the International Association for the Child's Right to Play (IPA), we are particularly disturbed by trends such as

1. Society's indifference to the importance of play.
2. Overemphasis on theoretical and academic studies in schools.
3. Inadequate environmental planning as manifest in the dehumanizing scale of settlements, inappropriate housing forms, and bad traffic management.

4. Increasing commercial exploitation of children through mass communication and mass production, leading to the deterioration of moral values and cultural traditions.
5. Inadequate preparation of children to cope with life in a rapidly changing society.
6. Increasing segregation of children in the community.
7. Constant exposure of children to war, violence, and destruction.
8. Overemphasis on unhealthy competition and "winning at all costs" in children's sports.

With increasing severity, inner-city children are being subjected to pressures and deprivations imposed by adult society, robbing them of opportunities for creative play essential for their healthy development. To counteract these alarming trends and their negative consequences, we propose the establishment of "safe-haven playgrounds," a type of playground that children can come to from early morning nearly every day of the year. These playgrounds would be loosely modeled on the adventure playground tradition.

Safe-haven playgrounds would be carefully supervised and would provide children with a range of activities and experiences that are not typically available to them in their homes and families. Children would attend these playgrounds after school, while parents are still at work, and on weekends and other nonschool days. Activities could include free play, instruction in special areas of high interest (model building, music, gardening, carpentry, computers, sewing, ceramics, animal care, etc.). Quiet spaces would be provided for school-related tutorials. Ages of users could range from the early elementary through high school levels, depending on how programs were organized.

Central to the idea of safe-haven playgrounds is to develop sites that are easily accessible to the community but protected from outside interference, social dangers, and vandalism by appropriate landscaping, barriers, and fencing. Here, a child could feel comfortable leaving a garden growing or a pet animal in a shelter or build a tree house or "clubhouse" without fear of them being vandalized. As in the adventure playground movement, tools and materials would be available to children so they could design and make their own toys and artifacts to fulfill their own needs. In other words, each child could have an ongoing self-initiated project or projects to work with daily. The educational aim would be to provide an environment that encourages independent thought and action among children — for some, an essential antidote to the excessive spoon feeding that takes place in the formal school system.

To implement this nonformal educational process, a new type of professional is needed. Such individuals would go through some of the same formal training as a regular classroom teacher but would receive additional background and practice in play theory, group relations, community development, counseling, and recreation. A special focus would be the hands-on play and learning activities that are impractical in school classrooms but would be most ideal for use in the safe-haven playgrounds.

This new type of nonformal educational professioinal would be modeled on the European play worker, *social pedagogue,* or *animator.* Their principal task would be to create an environment so compelling and inviting, so rooted in the things that children are inherently excited by, that children would choose the safe-haven playground as a more desirable alternative than television and other antisocial or development inhibiting activities.

An advantage of the safe-haven playground is that children would become aware that learning can occur in places other than the school. We are convinced, for instance, that hands-on activities like basic carpentry and cooking can teach most children as much about language, measurement, classification, and the use of basic math as most classroom and workbook exercises. Why? Because many children are more strongly motivated by self-chosen, hands-on tasks. Fundamental to the safe-haven playground concept is that learning is seen by children as part of their everyday life, providing them with tools with which to function in the world with maximum competence and enjoyment. This is especially important for the many disadvantaged children who must overcome the personal barrier of low esteem and be helped to see themselves as individuals of equal standing and ability to their peers.

The safe-haven playground curricula need to be open-ended and highly flexible. At the same time, they can be developed with guidelines that assure that children develop specific skills appropriate with their developmental levels. Individualized programs similar to those used in scouting merit badges might provide a useful model.

These ideas are in many respects like those of the educator and philosopher John Dewey who argued for the development of school curricula that would introduce children to a world they might have discovered by living on a traditional farm with experiences such as feeding and caring for animals, preserving food, using practical tools, and discovering nature.

Another goal of safe-haven playgrounds is to draw on members of the community to provide expert training. A local auto mechanic could run a class for older children on how to maintain and repair a car. A skilled cook living in the community could provide basic lessons in cooking. The possibilities are as wide and as varied as the resources of the community. Older children could be enlisted to teach younger children particular skills. Properly designed and implemented, the safe-haven playground could become a focal point for the development of local community identities, bringing a sense of shared community and meaning where it has not existed before.

**APPENDIX A**

**APPENDIX B**

**NOTES**

# INTERNATIONAL ASSOCIATION FOR THE CHILD'S RIGHT TO PLAY (IPA)

IPA is an international, nongovernmental organization founded in Denmark in 1961. It is an interdisciplinary organization and embraces in membership persons of all professions working for or with children. The organization works closely with many international NGOs and is recognized by the United Nations Economic and Social Council (ECOSOC) and by UNESCO and UNICEF as a nongovernmental organization with consultative status.

IPA is a human rights organization that shares a feeling of solidarity with children all over the world. IPA endorses the United Nations Convention on the Rights of the Child, particularly ARTICLE 31, which states that the child has a right to leisure, play, and participation in cultural and artistic activities. IPA promotes peace education through play and has been appointed as a United Nations Messenger of Peace.

IPA attempts to protect, preserve, and promote children's play as a means of ensuring the *maximum development* of every individual. Play stimulates creativity and the emotional, cognitive, and physical development of the whole child regardless of level of ability. Because children use play to explore their social and physical environment, it is a critical aspect of socialization and environmental education.

*Information within this appendix was abstracted from IPA's organizational literature.

IPA members believe that play, along with the basic needs of nutrition, health, shelter, and education, is vital for the development of the potential of all children and the protection and enhancement of their families, cultures, and communities. They believe that participation must be strengthened through play leadership and animation.

IPA members include professionals working in education, design, leisure time facilities, play programming, play leadership training, toys and play materials. Professional development and exchange take place through *Play-Rights*, the IPA quarterly magazine; *Play Journal*, the IPA professional journal; the IPA triennial international conference; regional and national conferences; seminars and study tours; and IPA Resources, London. Membership linkages with action groups in more than forty countries provide for an exchange of ideas and information about innovative, play-related nonformal education programs.

# IPA DECLARATION OF THE CHILD'S RIGHT TO PLAY

The IPA Declaration of the Child's Right to Play was originally produced in November 1977 at the IPA Malta Consultation held in preparation for the International Year of the Child (1979). It was revised by the IPA International Council in Vienna, September 1982, and Barcelona, September 1989. The IPA Declaration should be read in conjunction with ARTICLE 31 of the U.N. Convention on the Rights of the Child (adopted by the General Assembly of the United Nations, November 20, 1989), which states that the child has a right to leisure, play, and participation in cultural and artistic activities.

## What Is Play

*Children* are the foundation of the world's future.

*Children* have played at all times throughout history in all cultures.

*Play*, along with the basic needs of nutrition, health, shelter and education, is vital to develop the potential of all children.

*Play* is communication and expression, combining thought and action; it gives satisfaction and a feeling of achievement.

*Play* is instinctive, voluntary, and spontaneous.

*Play* helps children develop physically, mentally, emotionally and socially.

*Play* is a means of learning to live, not a mere passing of time.

## Alarming Trends Affecting Childhood

IPA is deeply concerned by a number of alarming trends and their negative impact on children's development:

- Society's indifference to the importance of play.
- Over-emphasis on theoretical and academic studies in schools.
- Increasing numbers of children living with inadequate provisions for survival and development.
- Inadequate environmental planning, which results in a lack of basic amenities, inappropriate housing forms, and poor traffic management.
- Increasing commercial exploitation of children, and the deterioration of cultural traditions.
- Lack of access for third world women to basic training in childcare and development.
- Inadequate preparation of children to cope with life in a rapidly changing society.
- Increasing segregation of children in the community.
- The increasing numbers of working children, and their unacceptable working conditions.
- Constant exposure of children to war, violence, exploitation and destruction.
- Over-emphasis on unhealthy competition and "winning at all costs" in children's sports.

## Proposals for Action

The following proposals are listed under the names of government departments having a measure of responsibility for children.

### Health

Play is essential for the physical and mental health of the child.

182

- Establish programmes for professionals and parents about the benefits of play from birth onwards.
- Ensure basic conditions (nutrition, sanitation, clean water and air) which promote the healthy survival and development of all children.
- Incorporate play into community programmes designed to maintain children's physical and mental health.
- Include play as an integral part of all children's environments, including hospitals and other institutional settings.

### Education

Play is part of education.
- Provide opportunities for initiative, interaction, creativity and socialisation through play in formal education systems.
- Include studies of the importance of play and the means of play provision in the training of all professionals and volunteers working with and for children.
- Strengthen play provision in primary schools to enhance learning and to maintain attendance and motivation.
- Reduce the incompatibilities between daily life, work and education by involving schools and colleges, and by using public buildings for community play programmes.
- Ensure that working children have access to play and learning opportunities outside of the system of formal education.

### Welfare

Play is an essential part of family and community life.
- Ensure that play is accepted as an integral part of social development and social care.
- Promote measures that strengthen positive relationships between parents and children.

- Ensure that play is part of community-based services designed to integrate children with physical, mental or emotional disabilities into the community.
- Provide safe play environments that protect children against abduction, sexual abuse and physical violence.

### *Leisure*

Children need opportunities to play at leisure.
- Provide time, space, materials, natural settings, and programmes with leaders where children may develop a sense of belonging, self-esteem, and enjoyment through play.
- Enable interaction between children and people of all backgrounds and ages in leisure settings.
- Encourage the conservation and use of traditional indigenous games.
- Stop the commercial exploitation of children's play, and the production and sale of war toys and games of violence and destruction.
- Promote the use of co-operative games and fair play for children in sports.
- Provide all children, particularly those with special needs, with access to a diversity of play environments, toys and play materials through community programmes such as pre-school play groups, toy libraries and play buses.

### *Planning*

The needs of the child must have priority in the planning of human settlements.
- Ensure that children and young people can participate in making decisions that affect their surroundings and their access to them.
- When planning new, or reorganizing existing developments, recognize the child's small size and limited range of activity.

- Disseminate existing knowledge about play facilities and play programmes to planning professionals and politicians.
- Oppose the building of high-rise housing and provide opportunities to mitigate its detrimental effects on children and families.
- Enable children to move easily about the community by providing safe pedestrian access through urban neighborhoods, better traffic management, and improved public transportation.
- Increase awareness of the high vulnerability of children living in slum settlements, tenements, and derelict neighborhoods.
- Reserve adequate and appropriate space for play and recreation through statutory provision.

### Affirmation

*IPA* is determined to sustain the momentum created by the International Year of the Child in 1979 to arouse world opinion for the improvement of the life of children and:

- Affirms its belief in the United Nations Convention on the Rights of the Child and endorses its belief in ARTICLE 31 of the Convention.
- Recognizes that the population of children in developing countries is three-quarters of the world's total child population, and that efforts directed at the promotion of education and literacy, and the stopping of environmental deprivation would improve the capacities of the poorest.
- Affirms its commitment to working with other national and international organizations to ensure basic conditions of survival for all children in order that they may fully develop as human beings.
- Acknowledges that each country is responsible for preparing its own course of public and political action in the light of its culture, climate and social, political and economic structure.
- Recognizes that the full participation of the community is essential in planning and developing programmes and services to meet the needs, wishes, and aspirations of children.

- Assures its co-operation with UN agencies and other international and national organizations involved with children.
- Appeals to all countries and organizations to take action to counteract the alarming trends which jeopardize children's healthy development and to give high priority to long term programmes designed to ensure for all time the Child's Right to Play.

# NOTES

## 1. Playgrounds: An Introduction

1. Jan Huizinga, *Homo Ludens* (Boston: Beacon Press, 1950), 1, 34–35.
2. John Dewey, *How We Think* (Boston: Heath, 1933), 212.
3. Jerome Bruner, "Play is Serious Business," *Psychology Today* 8, no. 8 (Jan. 1975): 83.
4. J. Johnson and J. Ershler, "Curricular Effects on the Play of Preschoolers," in *The Play of Children: Current Theory and Research*, ed. D. J. Pepler and K. Rubin, (Basel: Karger, 1982), 137.
5. George Maxim, *The Very Young* (California: Wadsworth, 1985), 146.
6. Mildred Parten, "Social Participation among Preschool Children," *Journal of Abnormal and Social Psychology* 33, no. 2 (Apr. 1932): 243–369.
7. Maxim, *Very Young*, 152–54.
8. S. Smilansky, *The Effects of Sociodramatic Play on Disadvantaged Children* (New York: Wiley, 1968).
9. Roland Barthes, *Mythologies* (New York: Hill and Wang, 1972), 54.
10. Louis Bowers, "Toward a Science of Playground Design: Principles of Design for Play Centers for All Children," *Leisure Today* (Oct. 1971): 21.
11. Joe L. Frost, "The American Playground Movement," *Childhood Education* (Feb. 1978): 176–82.
12. Ibid, 180.
13. Jane B. Moore and Aletha W. Bond, "Playgrounds: An Experience Center for Elementary Physical Education," *Journal of Physical Education and Recreation*, 46 (Jan. 1975): 21–25.
14. Frost, *American Playground Movement*, 178.
15. Robin C. Moore, Susan M. Goltsman, and Daniel S. Iacofano, *Play For All Guidelines: Planning, Design and Management of Outdoor Settings for All Children* (Berkeley: Calif. MIG Communication, 1992, 2d ed.).

16. Frost, 181.
17. Bill Michaelis, "Adventure Playgrounds: A Healthy Affirmation of the Rights of the Child," *JO-PER* (Oct. 1979): 55.
18. See the discussion of safety in chapter 6.

## 2. Historical Development and Evolution of Playgrounds

1. Jean McClintock and Robert McClintock, eds., *Henry Barnard's School Architecture* (1848; reprint, New York Teachers College Press, 1970), 209.
2. Ibid, 212.
3. Clarence Rainwater, *The Play Movement in the United States* (Chicago: Univ. of Chicago Press, 1922), 15.
4. Dominick Cavallo, *Muscles and Morals: Organized Playgrounds and Urban Reform, 1880–1920* (Philadelphia: Univ. of Pennsylvania Press, 1981), 23.
5. Ibid, 23. See also: Joe L. Frost, "Children's Playgrounds: Research and Practice," in *The Young Child at Play*, vol. 4 of *NAEYC, Reviews of Research*, ed. Greta Fein and Mary Rivkin (Washington; NAEYC, 1985–1986), 195.
6. Cavallo, *Muscles and Morals*, 23.
7. Rainwater, *Play Movement in the United States*, 61. See also Allen F. Davis, *Spearheads of Reform: The Social Settlement and the Progressive Movement, 1890–1914* (New York: Oxford Univ. Press, 1967), 63.
8. Jacob A. Riis, *Children of the Poor* (New York: Scribner, 1892), 186.
9. Ibid, 133.
10. Jacob A. Riis, "Playgrounds for City Schools," *The Century* 48 (Sept. 1894): 661.
11. Riis, "Playgrounds for City Schools," 666.
12. Rainwater, *Play Movement in the United States*, 49, 56.
13. Ibid, 57.
14. Cavallo, *Muscles and Morals*, 3.
15. Ibid.
16. Ibid, 155.
17. Ibid.
18. Quoted in Bill Michaelis, "Adventure Playgrounds: A Healthy Affirmation of the Rights of the Child," *JOPER* (Oct. 1979): 55.
19. Arvid Bengston, ed., *Adventure Playgrounds* (New York: Praeger, 1972), 15.
20. Ibid, 16.
21. Ibid.
22. Ibid, 17.
23. Michaelis, "Advenure Playgrounds," 57–58.

24. Bengston, *Adventure Playgrounds*, 8.
25. M. Paul Friedberg with Ellen Perry Berkleley, *Play and Interplay* (New York: Macmillan, 1970), 42.
26. Richard Dattner, *Design for Play* (New York: Van Nostrand Rienhold, 1969), 93.


### 3. Playgrounds: Theory and Research

1. Janet Lever, "Sex Differences in the Games Children Play," *Social Problems* 23, no. 4 (1976): 479–88.
2. Kathryn Borman, "Children's Interpersonal Relationships: Playground Games and Social Cognitive Skills," Final Report (Washington, D.C.: NIE, May 1981).
3. Judith Lyons, "Sex Differences in Aggressive and Withdrawn Behavior on the Playground," APA Annual Meeting, Canada, August 1984.
4. Kathryn Borman and Lawrence Kurdek, "Grade and Gender Differences in and the Stability and Correlates of the Structural Complexity of Children's Playground Games," *International Journal of Behavioral Development* 10, no. 2 (June 1987): 241–51.
5. Anthony Pelligrini and Jane Perlmutter, "Rough and Tumble Play on the Elementary School Playground," *Young Children* 43, no. 2 (Jan. 1988): 14–17.
6. Anthony Pelligrini, "Elementary School Children's Rough-and-Tumble Play," *Early Childhood Research Quarterly* 4, no. 2 (June 1989): 245–60.
7. Pia Bjorklid, "Children's Outdoor Environment from the Perspective of Environmental and Developmental Psychology," in *Children Within Environments*, ed. Tommy Garling and Jaan Valsiner (New York: Plenum Press, 1985), 91–106.
8. Joe L. Frost and E. Strickland, "Equipment Choices of Young Children during Free Play," in *When Children Play*, ed. J. L. Frost and S. Sunderlin (Wheaton, Md.: ACEI, 1985), 93–102.
9. Robin C. Moore, *Childhood's Domain* (Berkeley, Calif.: MIG Communications, 1990).
10. Joe L. Frost and Sheila Campbell, "Equipment Choices of Primary-Age Children on Conventional and Creative Playgrounds," in *When Children Play*, ed. J. L. Frost and S. Sunderlin (Wheaton, Md.: ACEI, 1985), 89–92.
11. Sheila Campbell and Joe L. Frost, "The Effects of Playground Type on the Cognitive and Social Play Behaviors of Grade Two Children," in *When Children Play*, ed. Joe L. Frost and S. Sunderlin, 81–88.
12. Carl P. Gabbard and Elizabeth LeBlanc, "Movement Activity Levels on Traditional and Contemporary Playground Structures," EDPS Document ED 198 082, 1980.
13. Craig Hart and Robert Sheehean, "Preschoolers' Play Behavior in Outdoor Environments: Effects of Traditional and Contemporary Playgrounds," *American Educational Research Journal* 23, no. 4 (Winter 1986): 668–78.

14. Carl Gabbard, *Playground Apparatus Experience and Muscular Endurance among Children*, ED 228 190, 1979.

15. Rita Yerkes, *A Playground That Extends the Classroom*, ERIC Document ED 239 802, 1982.

16. Catherine Poest, Jean Williams, David Witt, and Mary Atwood, "Physical Activity Patterns of Preschool Children," *Early Childhood Research Quarterly* 4 (1989): 367–76.

17. Alasdair Roberts, "Extraversion and Outdoor Play in Middle Childhood" *Educational Research* 21, no. 1 (Nov. 1978): 37–42.

18. Patricia Monighan-Nourot, Barbara Scales, and Judith Van Hoorn, *Looking at Children's Play* (New York: Teachers College Press, 1987), 100–14.

19. Kay Mogford, "The Play of Handicapped Children," in *Biology of Play*, ed. Barbara Tizard and David Harvey (London: Spastus International Medical Publications, 1977).

20. Ibid, 172–74.

21. Ibid, 176.

22. Ibid, 178–79.

23. Daniel Donder and John Nietupski, "Nonhandicapped Adolescents Teaching Playground Skills to Their Mentally Retarded Peers," *Education and Training of the Mentally Retarded* (Dec. 1981): 270–75.

24. Leopold Bellak and Maxine Antell, "An Intercultural Study of Aggressive Behavior on Children's Playgrounds," *American Journal of Orthopsychiatry* 44, no. 4 (July 1974): 503–11.

25. H. Allen Murphy, Michael J. Hutchison, and Jon Bailey, "Behavioral School Psychology Goes Outdoors: The Effect of Organized Games on Playground Aggression," *Journal of Applied Behavior Analysis* vol 16, no. 1 (Spring 1983): 29–35.

26. Liz Rothlein and Arlene Brett, "Children's, Teachers', and Parents' Perceptions of Play," *Early Childhood Research Quarterly* 2, no. 1 (Mar. 1987): 45–54.

## 4. Innovative Playgrounds: An International Survey

1. Robin C. Moore, *Childhood's Domain: Play and Place in Child Development*, (Berkeley, Calif.: MIG Communications, 1990).

2. Robin C. Moore, "Playgrounds at the Crossroads," in *Public Spaces and Places*, ed. Irwin Altman and Erwin Zube (New York: Plenum, 1989), 83–120.

3. Ibid, 103.

4. For further information about the Environmental Yard, see Robin C. Moore, "Before and After Asphalt: Diversity as an Ecological Measure of Quality in Children's Outdoor Environments," in *The Ecological Context of Children's Play*, ed. Marianne Bloch and Tony Pelligrini, (Norwood, N.J.: Ablex, 1989), 191–213; idem, "Plants as Play Props," in *Children and Vegetation*, special issue of *Children's Environments Quarterly* 6, no. 1 (Spring 1989): 3–6; idem "Like Diamonds Melting: Children's Play and Learning in Aquatic Settings," *Children's Environments Quarterly* 4, no. 2 (Summer 1987): 11–18; idem, "The Power of

Nature: Orientations of Girls and Boys toward Biotic and Abiotic Environments," *Children's Environments quarterly* 3 no. 3 (Fall 1986): 52–69; idem, "Animals on the Environmental Yard," *Children's Environments Quarterly* 1, no. 3 (Fall 1984): 43–51; idem, "Learning from the 'Yard'—Generating Relevant Urban Childhood Places," in *Play in Human Settlements,* ed. Paul F. Wilkinson (London: Croom Helm, 1979).

5.  David Driskell, Robin Moore, Daniel Iacofano, and Susan Goltsman, eds., *The Playful City Workbook* (Berkeley, Calif: MIG Communications, 1990).

6.  Ernest L. Boyer, *Ready to Learn: A Mandate for the Nation* (Princeton, N.J.: Carnegie Foundation for the Advancement of Teaching, 1991): 91–107.

## 5. Playgrounds and Exceptional Children

1.  Moore, Goltsman, Iacofano, *Play For All Guidelines,* xii–xiii.

2.  Pamela Leigh, "A Playground for All Children," *Parks and Recreation* 14, no. 5 (May 1979): 43.

3.  "Meeting the Playground Challenge," *The Exceptional Parent* 13, no. 2 (Apr. 1983): 14.

4.  Ibid., 14–15.

5.  Ibid., 16–18.

6.  Ibid., 19–20.

7.  George Bliss, Maurice Bateman, Guy Speisman, and Henry Haus, "Rotarians Respond to the Recreation Rights of Disabled Individuals in Mesa, Arizona," *CEPP Journal* (Jan. – Feb. 1983), 6–7.

8.  Ibid., 199–222.

9.  Sally B. Woodbridge, "Design by Community," *Landscape Architecture* 79, no. 8 (Oct. 1989): 83–84.

10. Ruth Cook, Annette Tessier, and Virginia Armbruster, *Adapting Curricula for Children with Special Needs* (Columbus, Ohio: Merrill, 1987), 148–50.

11. Leigh, *Playground for All Children,* 44.

12. P. Wehman, "Toward a Recreation Curriculum for Developmentally Disabled Persons" in *Recreation Programming for Developmentally Disabled Persons,* ed. P. Wehman (Baltimore: Univ. Park Press, 1979), 127.

13. Cook, Tessier, Armbruster, *Children with Special Needs,* 148–50.

14. Sean Murphy, "Don't Handicap Play Time for Disabled Children," *School Business Affairs* 54, no. 7 (July 1988): 48–53.

15. Tom Jambor and Richard Gargiulo, "The Playground: A Social Entity for Mainstreaming," *Journal of Physical Education, Recreation, and Dance* 58, no. 8 (Oct. 1987): 18–23.

16. William Servidio, "The Elimination of Mobility Barriers in Recreational Areas and Facilities," EDRS Document ED 157 863, 1978.

17. Richard Dattner, "Play without Barriers," *American School and University* 50, no. 1 (Sept. 1977): 61–62.

18. Lisa Carlson, "An Interdisciplinary Approach to the Design of Play Environments for Severely and Profoundly Retarded Institutionalized Residents" (Paper presented at the Annual International Convention of the Council for Exceptional Children, Dallas, Tex., Apr. 1979), 2–3.

19. Ibid., 4–8.

20. Ibid., 7–10.

21. Pamela Gillet, "Special Playground for Trainable Children," *The Pointer* 21, no. 3 (1977): 56.

22. Ibid., 59.

23. Dattner, "Play without Barriers," 64–65.

24. Murphy, "Don't Handicap Play Time," 50.

25. Jambor and Gariulo, "Playground," 21–22.

26. Dattner, "Play without Barriers," 63.

27. Goodwin Katzen, "Playgrounds for Everyone," *The Exceptional Parent* 11, no. 2 (Apr. 1981): 11–14.

28. Moore, Goltsman, and Iacofano, *Play for All Guidelines.*

## 6.  Playground Construction and Safety

1. Paul F. Wilkinson and Robert Lockhart, *Safety in Children's Formal Play Environments* (Report prepared for the Creative Play Committee of the Ontario Recreation Society and for the Ontario Ministry of Culture and Recreation, Toronto, 1976), 13.

2. Deborah K. Tinsworth and John T. Kramer, "Playground Equipment-Related Injuries and Deaths," Consumer Product Safety Commission, Directorate for Epidemiology, Washington, D.C. (Apr. 1990): 1–15.

3. Wilkinson and Lockhart, 14.

4. Ibid, 15.

5. Ibid.

6. National Safety Council, *Accident Facts 1986*, (Chicago National Safety Council, 1986).

7. Tinsworth and Kramer, 20.

8. Robin C. Moore, "Playgrounds at the Crossroads" in *Public Spaces and Places* ed. Irwin Altman and Erwin Zube (New York: Plenum, 1989).

9. W. Thomas Boyce, Sue Sobolewski, Lewis Sprunger, and Catherine Schaefer, "Playground Equipment Injuries in a Large, Urban School District," *American Journal of Public Health* 74, no. 9 (Sept. 1984): 984.

10. Moore, Goltsman, and Iacofano, *Play for all Guidelines*, chap. 11.

11. Frances Wallach, "Keep the Dragon Off Your Playground," *AS&U* (Jan. 1978): 27; Moore, Goltsman and Iacofano, *Play for all Guidelines*, chap. 9.

12. "NRPA Submits Proposed Playground Equipment Safety Standard," *Parks and Recreation* (Aug. 1976): 51.